Herald Express

SOUTH DEVON INN OUTINGS

15 Coast & Country Walks

Brian Carter

FOREST PUBLISHING

First published in 2006 by FOREST PUBLISHING,
Woodstock, Liverton, Newton Abbot, Devon TQ12 6JJ

British Library Cataloguing in Publication Data

A catalogue record for this book is available from the British Library.

ISBN 0 9549089 2 9

Forest Publishing

Editorial, layout and design by:

Mike Lang

Typeset by:

Carnaby Typesetting, Torquay, Devon TQ1 1EG

Printed and bound in Great Britain by:

The Latimer Trend Group, Plymouth, Devon PL6 7PY

Front cover: A view across the Teign estuary from the beer garden terrace of the Coombe Cellars Inn towards Bishopsteignton.

Courtesy of the Coombe Cellars Inn

Contents

Introduction

As a walkaholic I spend a lot of time in the South Devon countryside, from shore to moor; and the pleasure I find in a pint of blond beer, or real ale, and a tot or two of Irish whiskey, is well known to the regular readers of my daily *Herald Express* column.

After breaking a valve in the aorta artery, in the spring of 2002, I've been fighting my way back to fitness with the help of a pacemaker, a cardioversion to get rid of the irregular heartbeat, daily medication, the pushbike, and my walking boots.

My love of hiking and the open air hasn't diminished since a hyperactive boyhood. As a confirmed heretic hiker I'm happy to tramp along country roads and lanes, footpaths, and urban circuits.

I've done the west coast of Ireland, from Cork to Donegal; the coast and mountains of the Hebridean Island of Mull; the Snowdon Horseshoe Ridge; the Black Mountains, Cambrian Mountains, Brecon Beacons, and the Malverns; and the 15 Welsh mountains over 3,000 feet, 32 miles, in a day, several times.

Most of the hills and mountains on the west side of the UK have seen the soles of my boots, as the upland pilgrimage, which began in 1952, when I was fifteen, continues.

Today I'm happy with my *Inn Outings*, over a variety of distances and terrain. Apart from the physical rewards, and working up a lager thirst, a good walk brings me closer to nature. But in town I like the smells wafting from chip shops, pubs and bakeries. Then there are the wildlife cameos of coast and country.

Encounters with animals and humans can spice a good hike: I've been yapped at by moody magpies in suburbia; hissed at by an old woman who resented me watching her chihuahua leaving a deposit on Paignton Green; and growled at by winos and junkies flopped out on park or prom benches. But yesterday's backstreet lad wasn't impressed.

Whenever possible I like to start and end my walks at a pub. Then there's the chance of finding a Dusky Ruth lookalike behind the bar, Mozart on the jukebox (dream on), and the glow of a pub fire to set the seal on a winter hike.

I'm convinced that walking solo, in pairs, or with a small group of friends or relatives, is good for body and soul. The red cliffs of South Devon (with a dash of lime); lark song over urban-fringe countryside; sunset, sunrise, and lights coming on in a village as dusk closes – out walking you find a lot happening.

A hike on home ground or new territory can provide an escape from stress and worry. Yes, nature and green places have healing qualities. At the end of a few hours in the fresh air it's good to hear the Devon accent as you sample your first beer of the day in the pub of your choice.

So, I like walking for all it can offer. It's a cheap way to keep fit or get fit, and it's damned good fun.

* Anyway, strong, reliable footwear is a real asset to the safety factor, especially in winter conditions or on a coastal footpath after rain.
* Certain sections of narrow country roads can be busy, so take care, and if you are a member of a group walk in single file, facing the oncoming traffic.
* Read the walks carefully and consult the relevant Ordnance Survey Map, or A to Z Street Map, before you set off. This is essential.
* GRADING:–
  A – Easy. B – Not so easy. C – More demanding. D – Demanding.

THE 15 WALKS

Walk No.	Walk Name	Grade
1.	The English Riviera Trail (6 miles).	B
2.	The Maidencombe – Brunel Wood Circuit ($3^1/_2$ miles).	B
3.	Enjoying the Torbay Proms (7 miles).	C
4.	Dart Estuary and Farmland Circuit ($4^1/_2$ miles).	B
5.	Paignton Liberty Lady Circuit (4 miles).	A
6.	High on the Haldons Circuit (4 miles).	C
7.	Lighthouse and Lyte House Circuit ($3^1/_2$ miles).	A

(Distances given are approximate.)

Brian Carter
March 2006

1. The English Riviera Trail

Start and finish point: Torquay – The Hole in the Wall pub (SX 921 635).
Distance: About 6 miles.
Degree of difficulty: Grade B.
Route: The Hole in the Wall pub; The Strand; Corbyn's Head; Livermead; Hollicombe Head; Marine Parade; Preston prom; Paignton prom; Paignton pier; and reverse the route to the Hole in the Wall pub.

Leaving the Hole in the Wall pub, in Park Lane, I turned left into Torwood Street and came on just past the Clock Tower to cross over the junction of Torwood Street and Victoria Parade at the traffic lights. Then I walked along the harbourside to the quay called Vaughan Parade.

It was a breezy, cloudy, winter morning. Yachts, pleasure boats, and launches were moored in the Old Harbour, and I had close-ups of the craft in Torquay Marina as I loped along Princess Parade.

Beyond the Pavilion Shopping Centre I walked the broad prom. On the right were the lawns, flowerbeds and fountains of Princess Gardens, with the Princess Theatre and Princess Pier a bit further on. A yob gull just missed my head with a sloppy dollop, while his mates yodelled and cackled like witches on a hen-party binge.

Over the A379 Torbay Road to the right were the limestone crags and gardens of Rock Walk. Stunning Bay views were opening up and the dark sandstone profile of Corbyn's Head waited at the far end of Torre Abbey Sands.

At the pedestrian bridge I came down onto the seafront. The tide was low and a few dog walkers moved briskly on Abbey Sands. Most of the seafront strollers were well wrapped up. But I wondered why the black-headed gulls on the sea wall were laughing.

Then a short, fat chap, squashed into a tight-fitting tracksuit, jogged by, marginally slower than an overweight tortoise learning to walk upright on its back legs. He looked like a character out of BBC 3's *Little Britain*. Mystery solved.

At the end of Corbyn's Beach I came up the cliff steps and path onto Corbyn's Head. Across the road was the big, multi-storey apartment block, next to the aptly named Grand Hotel.

I walked across the lawns, past the rest shelter and public toilets, taking in more of those great Bay views, with Brixham and Berry Head away to the south-east. The sun was breaking

through. The sea glittered and I was on the pavement, close to the sea wall above Livermead Beach.

Traffic roared by. On the opposite side of the A3022 road were the Livermead House Hotel and Cockington Lane. But I was coming up by the Livermead Cliff Hotel for a good climb between the mix of bungalows, hotels, guest houses, and other properties, to the bus shelter. Then it was on round the bend, where the main road crossed the railway, to the brow of the hill for the descent into Hollicombe.

On the left, above the railway embankment, scarred with fox and badger runs, gulls and starlings provided the bustle, watched by a buzzard in a tree on a nameless headland. The old bird of prey may have been a distant relative of the Queen. He had that 'We are not amused' expression on his face. The lightweight binoculars, I carry in my rucksack, gave me an intimate close-up.

In the lap of the combe I came through the big wrought-iron gates into Hollicombe Park, where the cast of the wildlife cabaret on the big round pond was swans, mallard and seabirds.

Palms and exotic plants in the shrubberies looked cold and fed up. But I was happy to walk the path to the right, up to the metal gate onto another path, for the left turn which brought me over the railway onto Hollicombe Head, where I turned right.

The manicured lawn ended at songbird-haunted hedges; and I stood in the grass for a while, savouring the views. The vision of coastland from Churston's woods to Brixham and Berry Head always brings a warm flush to my spirit. And that's true – not goofball romanticism.

Down below Hollicombe Head's sandstone cliffs the rocks, skerries, and shallows bring in the seabirds and birdwatchers, according to the season. Among the avian attractions are wintering black-necked and Slavonian grebes; divers, purple sandpipers, and turnstones. But it was enough for me to hear the bleeping and piping of oystercatchers, and watch gulls mooching about on the shellfish trail.

A narrow flight of steps brought me onto Marine Parade for another prom stomp; and soon I was passing the refreshment kiosk to hurry into the public loo.

Continuing the walk, I followed the prom above Preston Sands

The prom above Preston Sands bathed in early evening sunshine.
Author

for more easy hiking past the Boathouse Restaurant and on round the bend that saw me onto the pavement beside Marine Drive.

After coming below the holm-oaks of the Redcliffe Hotel I passed Villa Marina and was on Paignton prom, which is called Eastern Esplanade on the road maps. As a Paigntonian this was home territory.

The North Green was to the right, and herring gulls and black-headed gulls (minus their dark, breeding-season hoods) were tap-dancing on the cropped turf. No, they weren't auditioning for a Walt Disney movie. They were conning earthworms into thinking it was raining. A downpour brings the invertebrates wriggling to the surface, where they become the birds' takeaways.

Strolling along the seafront towards the pier, I indulged my enthusiasm for the local marine scene. But a moment later I was behind a large, elderly woman who was puffing on a fag. I coughed, she turned, glared, growled, and puffed on.

Like the look she gave me, the weather was chilly. But in fleece, shorts and walking boots I was comfortable. My rucksack wasn't heavy and there I was at my Paignton pier turning point. Built in 1878 for local businessman Mr Hyde Dendy, it's a familiar landmark on today's South West Coast Path. Ahead was the Apollo cinema complex, and looking out to sea I took in the complete view.

Beyond Roundham Head the cliffs ended dramatically at Berry Head's profile. Across the Bay, in the opposite direction, I could see Hope's Nose, Thatcher Rock, and Ore Stone. Vessels of all sizes moved up or down the Channel. At the north end of the Torbay horseshoe Torquay's buildings were Mediterranean – impressive on their hills.

A bottle of sparkling mineral water later I was ready to retrace my steps, something I never flinch from as a heretic hiker. Reversing the route, when a circuit isn't on the cards, gives you a new set of views. And that was the bonus of my return to Torquay Harbour, The Strand, the Clock Tower, and Park Lane where the Hole in the Wall was waiting.

The tucked-away, historic building is Torquay's oldest inn, dating from about 1540. Inside I found a low-beamed ceiling, inglenooks, and pleasant lighting.

The entrance to the Hole in the Wall.

Chris Carter

Like so many pubs it reminded me of what this sort of place meant to our ancestors; and the English inn still has a colourful role in the country's social life. Over the centuries it has flourished under a variety of names – tavern, alehouse, inn, public house, victualling house, roadhouse, coffee house, and hotel.

Individual pubs brew their own atmosphere. OK, inn has a warm ring to it; but all successful pubs have to move with the times in many ways.

Yet, in spirit, the Hole in the Wall wasn't that far from Chaucer's The Tabard, and the Old Bull and Bush on London's Hampstead Heath.

The attractive, comfortable restaurant specialises in seafood dishes, and among the half dozen real ales on draught was Spitfire, one of my favourites. Traditional pumped beers, ciders, lagers, and whiskies were also available, along with plenty of tempting meals on the lunchtime menu.

No wonder the Hole in the Wall was once popular with smugglers. But I was content to settle for a jacket potato and prawn Marie Rose, with a pint of Spitfire, in that friendly atmosphere.

The author behind the bar – for a change!

Chris Carter

2. The Maidencombe – Brunel Wood Circuit

Start and finish point: Maidencombe – Pay-and-display car park (SX 927 684).
Distance: About $3^1/_2$ miles.
Degree of difficulty: Grade B.
Route: The pay-and-display car park, Maidencombe; the lane; Goat Path; Valley of the Rocks; Watcombe Beach Road; Steps Cross; Brunel Wood; Rock House Lane; and the Thatched Tavern.

It was a hot summer's day and I was leaving Maidencombe pay-and-display car park to come up the narrow country road past the Thatched Tavern, old cottages and old farms. The Courthouse, on the bend, has been there for about 600 years. In the garden is the celebrated Judas Tree, imported as a sapling from Lebanon around 1500. It's very beautiful under spring blossom.

On I went past Steep Hill and Brim Hill to climb the very steep lower part of Rock House Lane. But it wasn't long before I came to the wide path on the bend to the left. It was signposted: 'Watcombe – Coast Path'.

Well, it turned out to be a lovely, winding farm track-cum-lane, with many ups and downs on the climb towards high ground.

The wild meadows on the left were cirl bunting territory. These little songbirds are quite rare, but a few pairs breed between the lane and the clifftop shrubs. They are seed-eaters and the species originated from the Mediterranean area. So, many are the victims of hard winter weather.

Not so long ago just over 300 pairs, the entire cirl bunting population of the UK, were located along the South Devon coast. You can find a description of them in any good bird book. But you are more likely to hear one than see it, although the birds can sometimes be found in large suburban gardens with plenty of cover.

The cirl bunting delivers a brief, tuneless, trilling rattle, and a wrenlike churr if it's scared or angry. But I'm not going to give you a lecture on ornithology. Nature study embraces almost everything, from seeding grasses to birds, beetles, badgers and beer garden bipeds. Enough said.

The track brought me through the trees to the top of the Goat Path. Before me was a combe full of mainly mature sycamores. It was the Valley of the Rocks, and rising above the woodland to the right, almost hidden by foliage, was the great sandstone dome of Giant Rock; at 150 feet high this is South Devon's Yosemite. The face is pockmarked with caves and scarred with gullies.

At the foot of vertical cliffs the Goat Path was narrow, and high above the valley. So, descend with care, using the handrail.

Coming down the rough, red steps I was reversing what was once The Cream Tea Trail taken by my grandparents' generation. In the summers between the world wars couples took their Sunday afternoon walks from St Marychurch to Maidencombe for cream teas at Rose Cottage.

In the late spring and early summer the steep sandstone bank above the path is covered with culinary and herbal plants like the wild cabbage, wild onion and wild carrot; marjoram, salad burnet, and thyme.

Leaving the wildflower rock faces at the bottom of the path, I entered the wood to come along the broad ride of baked red soil below Giant Rock. It brought me past the old pits where terracotta clay was once quarried for thriving businesses like Watcombe Pottery.

On I went, able to ignore any signposts aimed at walkers looking for the Coast Path. Then I was in the car park, and near the entrance on the right-hand side at the top were some strange-looking plants called field horsetails.

These dull green, bristly, 'loo brushes' once dominated the world's vegetation. Spore-bearing, they have root systems that can reach depths of about 60 feet.

In distant geological times horsetails were 100 feet tall and food for dinosaurs. Their remains are fossil fuel, in other words gas or coal.

Now, whenever someone starts talking about prehistoric creatures and plants, I recall Dad's outburst in my kid days, following his serious attack of 'the runs' after Mam had loosened his bowels with one of her awful mixed meat curries.

Returning, pale and shaking from his tenth visit to the outside lav, he looked at me and said: 'Thanks to your mother's cooking I've got a complaint that gave certain prehistoric monsters their name'.

'And that is?' Mam sighed, waiting for it.

'Diner's-sore-arse', Dad grinned, reaching for the whisky bottle.

Leaving the car park, I came up the hill on narrow Watcombe Beach Road, keeping to the right to face oncoming traffic. At the top I nipped across the busy B3199 without taking any chances. Then it was down Moor Lane, past Maylands School, to Steps Cross and the right turn into Steps Lane. Ignoring the first turning left into Brunel Avenue, I came left when the avenue cropped up again, very soon.

A few yards away to the right was the footpath into Brunel Wood, which was named after the famous GWR engineer Isambard Kingdom Brunel, 1806–1859. He had created Watcombe Park, but died with the building of his nearby house, Brunel Manor, still in its early stages.

It was sweltering hot but I felt good in T-shirt, shorts and leather boots. A few birds called as I came up the path, past the first of the Brunel water gardens, long dried up and buried under the greenery.

There are plenty of paths to take you through the wood. But my route, bearing right, gave me the chance to make a short detour, down to the left, and stop to admire the wooden sculptures centred on the tall 'totem pole' in the grassy hollow. On this circuit many elderly walkers may welcome the chance to loiter with content.

Called Brunel's Dance, the tall sculpture celebrates the engineer's achievements. Among the 19th century characters are Queen Victoria and a railwayman, as well as bridges, boats, and locomotives, all of which are the work of sculptor Keith Barrett.

At the base are three separate 'totem figures', like characters out of *Alice in Wonderland*. One is Brunel, and the other two symbolise fire and water, which together produce steam – the driving force of the Victorian Age.

Returning to the baked-mud path, that widened as it climbed the slope, I looked at some of the big trees. The most spectacular is the Monterey Cypress, a huge candelabrum with an amazing upward sweep of boughs. It's about 150 years old.

The wood is a half-wild park with its variety of mature trees and network of paths. The brick gulley in the centre, hidden by stone chippings and vegetation, once fed water to the lower water garden. Ladybirds were on the wing and there was evidence of badger activity. Brunel Manor could be glimpsed through the trees on the right.

Emerging from the wood, I turned right into Seymour Drive and swung right through the gap beside the gate to come along the path next to the wood. Then I ignored the left and right turn-offs and went straight on among the buildings for another right turn that brought me to the B3199 again. I crossed it with all the guile of a seasoned walker, well-versed in the code of highway Russian Roulette, and came down Rock House Lane.

Architecturally speaking this lane runs through a corner of Victorian England. The big houses are fine examples of 19th century, privileged-class development, with Langley Manor a masterpiece.

Striding downhill, on the single-track road, I paused briefly for a chat with a hedgerow grey squirrel. Fortunately there were no human witnesses about!

But walking on I was hit on the head by a wasp that became tangled in my hair. Half a dozen ramblers, coming up the road, gave me a wide berth as I cursed and jigged about, shaking my bonce in my efforts to evict the unwelcome lodger before it could sting me. For a moment or two I must have resembled one of Mr Barrett's eccentric figures come to life, especially as my shorts and T-shirt could have been mistaken for Victorian underwear!

Operation successful, to the applause of the audience, I hiked on between the leafy hedges and handsome old stone walls. Over

The Thatched Tavern and its award-winning beer garden.
Courtesy of the Thatched Tavern

the farmland was a great view of Lyme Bay; and on my right was Rock House, once the home of Rudyard Kipling.

The famous writer and his wife spent a year there. But Kipling didn't get on with the stuffy businessmen of Torquay. He found their po-faced pomposity irritating and depressing.

Well, beyond authors behaving badly (sniff-sniff), every time I do this walk I'm conscious of the steep descent to the sea, in the tradition of so many South Devon lanes. Then there was the wayside wildflower show, butterfly dance, and the furtive hedgetop movements of birds.

Passing the house called Ferndale, I swung left around the steep, blind bend and continued on beyond the beginning of Brim Hill into the heart of the small community of Maidencombe. It was lunchtime and the Thatched Tavern was busy.

The tavern, with its white walls, weathered thatch, handsome interior, and award-winning beer garden, is a classic example of a pub from the traditional rural mould. It looks like a big cottage and has plenty of customer appeal. I've dined there and can vouch for the quality of the cuisine, drink, and service.

There is the bar, a non-smoking bar, and the restaurant. You have the opportunity to sample good bitters, a couple of lagers, whiskies, a selection of wines, cider, cask-conditioned real ales and beers. Food ranges from à la carte meals to bar snacks.

It was good to sit in the cool bar and enjoy a pint of real ale and a bar snack sandwich.

For nearly 50 years I've travelled far to visit some famous inns. High on the list are the Prospect of Whitby, Wapping Wall, London; the Falcon, Stratford-on-Avon; the George and Pilgrim, Glastonbury; the Hop Pole, Tewkesbury; Haunch of Venison, Salisbury; King's Arms, Dorchester; the Sun, Canterbury; and many others.

A lot of South Devon pubs maintain that tradition of hospitality, well-kept beer, and good pub grub, which is the hallmark of quality, nationwide.

✳ ✳ ✳ ✳ ✳

3. Enjoying the Torbay Proms

Start and finish point: Paignton – The Flagship 2 for 1 Pub (SX 894 604).
Distance: About 7 miles.
Degree of difficulty: Grade C.
Route: The Flagship 2 for 1 Pub, Apollo complex, Paignton prom; Paignton Harbour; Roundham Head; Goodrington; Three Beaches Head; Broadsands; Churston Point, and back.

The December morning was bright but hazy on Paignton's Eastern Esplanade. That's still 'the Prom' to vintage locals.

The Flagship 2 for 1 Pub is part of the Apollo complex. The stylish, white, modern building is a well-known feature of Paignton's seafront scene. It was built in 1999.

Leaving the pub I came to the right, under Shoreline Cafe. Sea

The Flagship 2 for 1 Pub.

Chris Carter

and sky were blue, and lots of starlings were settling on the cafe roof to do some carol singing in a Gaelic so old only St Francis would understand it.

The rising tide was bringing in the smell of salt water and seaweed. Where Tor Bay met the Channel, Thatcher Rock and Ore Stone were attracting seabirds off Torquay's Hope's Nose.

At the harbour end of the prom and South Green I walked past the elegant, cream facade of the Paignton Club House to come round the bend below the thatched cottages.

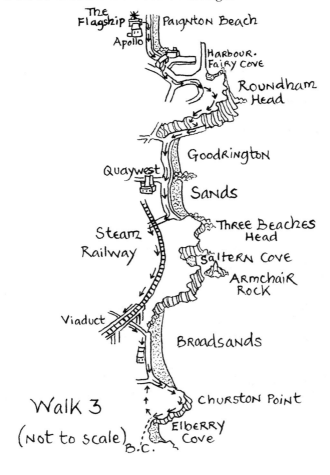

The archway of the Harbour Light Restaurant brought me to Paignton Harbour. Small craft were at their moorings and a variety of vessels were on the quay, ready for the treatment that would smarten them up for the tourist season. It brought back memories of childhood and wartime walks with my Gran. Passing the public toilets, after I had turned left at the top of the right-hand slope, a lot of local history hit me. The WC cottage was once the coastguard station. The harbour was built in 1838, and was taken over by Paignton Council in 1936, the year Miss Stella Gale became the only female harbour 'master' in the UK.

The Harbour Light Restaurant and Paignton Harbour.

Author

From the clifftop, near the old coastguard station, my ancestors would have seen the local fishing fleet set sail, in early March, on the Newfoundland Cod Run. That annual venture lasted from the Middle Ages into the early 20th century. Dried and salted cod went to markets in Britain and on the continent.

Yes, the old trading port of Paignton is pickled in history. My memories go back to the 1940s, and I haven't forgotten the spectacle of warships and landing craft in the Bay as the Allied

Fleet prepared for D-Day.

Walking past the harbour I came on for the left turn into Cliff Road, and the short pavement stretch to Roundham Head Park, up on the left. It was just beyond the uninspired apartment block architecture above Fairy Cove.

The weather was mild. A few OAPs were on the pathside benches, reading newspapers and paying no attention to the jackdaws busking on the lawns. One of the birds had obviously cast a spell over the others. Maybe he was the Brendan Behan of daws, turning on a verbal firework display after an all-night whisky and Guinness session.

Beyond the group of tall pines the path led me into some great Bay views, with Berry Head at the south-eastern end of the Torbay 'horseshoe', and Hope's Nose at the other. OK, I know I'm always on about the scenic quality of the home territory. But I'm not apologising. This is one of the most beautiful bays in Britain, and born-and-bred I'm always prepared to advertise its merits.

Distances were soft in the haze. Before me the low, red headlands and wooded coast went on to meet Brixham's limestone. And a few moments later I made a footpath-and-steps descent of the hanging Roundham Cliff Gardens: my Grandfather and Dad, both carpenters, were part of the big workforce that completed the building of this major attraction in 1931.

The prom saw me onto the seafront above Goodrington North Sands. On the beach a few dog walkers were enjoying the sea air.

Following the prom, past Young's Park and its boating lakes, I came by the Inn on the Quay on the headland above Middle Stone – the rocks and skerries which separate Goodrington North and South Sands.

From the next prom I could see the flumes of Quaywest Water Park. Memories swarmed. Among them were the bucket-and-spade holiday scenes of post-war summers, with Punch getting head-butted by Judy. And Peter Pan's Playground still registers in Hollywood technicolour behind my eyes.

At the end of the prom, above South Sands, I went under the railway bridge and up the steps to the left, onto the continuation of the South West Coast Path. No problems. All you have to do is follow it and the acorn logo, and it brings you to Broadsands.

On one side was the Paignton and Dartmouth Steam Railway: on the other, the bungalow gardens of Three Beaches. Time to enjoy the walking for its own sake.

The path saw me past Three Beaches Head and on above Saltern Cove. All the promontories and coves from Corbyn's Head to Churston Point are one long site of Special Scientific Interest (SSSI).

I've visited Saltern Cove from the late 1940s onwards, doing some marine nature study. The rock pools are home to shrimps, snakelocks, anemones, blennies, starfish, the odd conger eel, and crabs. In the distant past I recall my first encounter with a devil's crab and its big red eyes.

If you visit the cove look, learn, but take nothing away.

Oystercatchers piped and I could imagine what was going on among the red weeds, kelp, and sea lettuce as I came past the grassy dome of Sugar Loaf Hill, on the right. Before me was the railway viaduct. Looking back, I enjoyed the coastal panorama as three joggers went by, staring straight ahead. Then it was down the steps, on past the holiday camp, with the railway on the left, its embankment covered with fox-coloured bracken.

Below the next headland was Devil's Armchair, which is now called Armchair Rock on the maps. Umm, yes. Is this another example of political correctness? Have the authorities decided to get rid of the Devil in the name because they don't want to encourage Satanists and upset churchgoers?

Soon I was above the clifftops of Shell Cove and Crystal Cave. It was another of those pleasant, switchback hikes, with houses on the right and the Bay on the left. Through the hush I could hear the slap and fizz of waves breaking and retreating.

Then there was a descent of 120 steps that dumped me on the footpath below the viaduct. Half a dozen fieldfares flew across the farmland as I came down to the prom above Broadsands, where I swung right.

Every so often I paused to look out to sea where bottle-nose dolphins are sometimes seen in the shallow, offshore water. Inland were the two viaducts which carry the steam trains to Kingswear and back. But the big car park, which is rarely more than a quarter full, was once a marsh and ley, and a very important migratory point for birds. Most of it was destroyed in the 1960s. But there are rumours it will be returned to its former wildlife glory.

Yes, and after my sixth lager this evening I know I'll see pigs flying around Berry Head lighthouse … honest.

At the end of the prom I came up through the small metal gate onto Churston Point for another set of Bay views. The path followed the clifftops beside the pitch-and-putt golf course, with the ruins of a barn on the right. And it wasn't long before I was looking down on Elberry Cove, with Marridge Woods beyond.

Then I turned right and came down Elberry Lane, past Elberry Farm, and along the prom at Broadsands again for the return to the Apollo. The new views, and prospect of a snack and a cool beer at the end of the hike, were all the 'fuel' I needed.

The Flagship 2 for 1 Pub was the first pub in Torbay to ban smoking. It has a spacious, beautifully furnished bar, with large wooden tables throughout. This means families, or groups of friends, can eat and drink in comfort.

There are wooden beams and chairs, low lighting, a long counter, and a separate corner area just for drinkers.

The Wacky Warehouse, children's playroom, is on the right as you come in the main entrance off Esplanade Road. The Sundeck, on the pub's roof, is the beer garden where customers can sit and eat and drink in the summer.

The 2 for 1 in the Flagship's name is a direct reference to the special food offer. Customers order two full-price adult main course meals on the menu, and get the cheaper one free.

I had a look at the listed starters; hot and spicy meals; Chinese; Italian; grills; and chicken favourites; as well as the traditionals, salads, and light options. There was also a Kids' Menu.

Carlsberg, Carlsberg Export, Carling, Stella Artois, Guinness, Tetleys, and Strongbow were on draught. A large selection of wines lined the shelves; and the spirits included Jamesons Irish Whiskey.

The Flagship is a New Millennium concept of the pub. But with Christmas near I knew old traditions were bound to surface. At that moment, though, I was thinking of lager and one of the starters. My choice was the loaded potato wedges, with sour cream dip, and a pint of sparkling Carlsberg Export.

It was a tasty finale to the Torbay Proms.

4. Dart Estuary and Farmland Circuit

Start and finish point: Kingswear (SX 882 510).
Distance: About $4^1/_2$ miles.
Degree of difficulty: Grade B.
Route: The Lower Ferry slipway; Alma Steps; Higher Brownstone; Kingston; and the Mount Ridley Road back to the Ship Inn.

I was in Kingswear, the village on the hillside above the lower reaches of the Dart estuary. Thousands of people pass through it, mainly in the spring and summer, en route to Dartmouth across the water, via the Lower Vehicle Ferry. But the community has a charm of its own, although some of it is tucked away, like the Ship Inn.

Down by the quay, the station of the Paignton and Dartmouth

Steam Railway is a feature of riverside life, and a popular tourist attraction.

That morning I saw what looked like crab boats coming in. The weather was typical for late winter: a week of heavy rain had given way to a sunny spell. But I wasn't kidding myself. I had no intention of walking the Coast Path along the clifftops. It would be too muddy and I wasn't in the mood for skidding about on my butt. I was there for the pleasure of a modest hike, a farmland vision of that corner of South Devon, and an inn at the end of it all.

At the bottom of Fore Street I came to the slipway of the Lower Vehicle Ferry, watching the ferry ploughing across the estuary. Apart from the marina, the river between Kingswear and Dartmouth is a great yacht anchorage, with craft of all sizes at their moorings.

I was ready for the hike; and while the memories took over I tightened my bootlaces. I had done the South West Coast Path, from Paignton to Kingswear, several times. But I also enjoy the short, mainly inland circuit that begins and ends at the village.

So off I went through the arch on the left that brought me to Alma Steps, and the South West Coast Path signpost. At the top I turned right to follow the path which is actually a single-track road, with great views of Dartmouth over the estuary, against the hills of the South Hams.

A bit further on were Halftide Rock, One Gun Point, Castle Point, and Dartmouth Castle. I was walking under the trees at a steady pace, watched by a flock of finches and a pair of crows.

The winding route brought me down to the big white house called Brookhill. At the next signpost I took the path marked: 'Brownstone, three-quarters of a mile'. The Coast Path was also signposted but, despite the stunning coastal views, I wasn't tempted. I wanted to look at the farmland I had discovered in 1947, during my last year at primary school.

The Brownstone trail passed The Grange and Home Cottage above the wooded coastland. Kingswear Castle and Mill Bay were down below. Then I crossed the footbridge over the stream to climb the steep, rough track. Care is needed, especially after rain.

Conditions improved at Crockers Cottage, and the long haul

continued to the outbuildings of Brownstone. On the hillside to the right was the Day Mark, erected in 1864 as a daytime navigational aid to Channel shipping heading for Dartmouth.

By New Cottages the road passed the National Trust car park at Higher Brownstone, and Coleton Barton Farm above Coleton Fishacre House and Gardens, which are open to the public. Once the home of the D'oyly Cartes, Coleton Fishacre is now owned by the National Trust.

Well, the farmland views were a treat. At the crossroads I turned left and walked up past the handful of houses at Kingston. Behind me was the drive leading to Coleton Fishacre. On the right was the lane that liberated more memories. It leads to the coast and deep into my past.

In the late 1940s and early '50s a few friends and I prowled around the sea cliffs, looking for the easiest sites to harvest herring gulls' eggs. Hitler's war had started it all. During the food shortage springs our mothers used gulls' eggs in cake mixes and omelettes. And, despite the mythology, they didn't have a fishy tang: the taste was strong, but we never had them boiled.

At the next junction I took the left-hand fork opposite Scabbacombe Lane which runs to Woodhuish Farm and Man Sands. Gaps in the flail-mowed hedge revealed views of the

Channel and the Day Mark. But my hope of seeing the first house martins back home for the breeding season came to nothing.

Never mind. I knew spring would cover the hedgebanks with wildflowers to join the hardy ones which bloom in winter; and there was still the chance of catching a burst or two of larksong. No wonder a couple of upright badgers were slow-jiving in the corner of a field, watched by half a dozen rabbits.

Then I was on the Mount Ridley Road, confronted by a stunning vision of Dartmouth to the right, with Britannia Royal Naval College huge on the hillside above the estuary. Completed in 1905, the college was named after a three-decker hulk that was home to embryo naval officers.

Dartmouth and the Dart estuary.

Author

The sheen of fine weather lay on the Dart valley. The lower flanks of the hills across the water were hidden by houses. Townstal church was at the top, with green hills beyond; and I was passing Fountain Violet Farm on the left.

Some contemporary housing development registered at Kingswear Park Apartments. And it occurred to me that the quiet

The Ship Inn, as seen from outside Kingswear Hall.
Mike Goodearl

The interior of the Ship Inn.
Mike Goodearl

road, winding downhill and providing more estuary views, was better walked alone, with no verbal distractions.

Moments later the route brought me to Castle Road and onto Church Hill in Kingswear. Just past the Church of Saint Thomas of Canterbury I went to the right up narrow Higher Street; and there was the cream and blue facade of the Ship Inn, opposite Kingswear Hall. It wasn't far from the Lower Vehicle Ferry slipway.

The 15th century Heavitree House is medieval small. Opening the door, I found myself in a cosy little bar, with low lighting and a beamed ceiling. The restaurant was up the steps, not far from the log fire.

The Ship has real ales, a couple of lagers, and a choice of whiskies. The board behind the bar advertised a wide variety of meals.

The pub was brewing its own warmth, and it was good to sit on a bar stool with a glass of beer, listening to the crackle of logs burning. It was half an hour before my son was due to pick me up in Fore Street for the lift home.

The Ship had provided the ideal full stop to another of my shorter walks. My Celtic mother would have loved it.

CARTER

5. Paignton Liberty Lady Circuit

Start and finish point: Paignton – The Flagship 2 for 1 Pub (SX 894 604).
Distance: About 4 miles.
Degree of difficulty: Grade A.
Route: The Flagship 2 for 1 Pub, Apollo complex, Paignton prom; Victoria Park; Oldway Mansion and Gardens; Hollicombe Park; the beach, proms, and the Flagship pub again.

It was June 21, the official first day of summer. At noon I left the Apollo at the doors of the pub and Wacky Warehouse and came over the pedestrian crossing to swing right along Esplanade Road. After passing The Spinning Wheel and Park Hotel I turned left into Garfield Road. At the top, on the sharp bend, was the entrance to Victoria Park, with the multi-storey car park on the left.

I crossed the road cautiously and once I was in the park I followed the right-hand path beside the stream. Gulls were strutting their thing on the lawn and, at the same time, mallard splashed about on the water, macho drakes swopping insults while the ducks looked at them and shook their heads. Some had youngsters with them.

Coming under the railway bridge, I saw the Children's Play Area ahead on the left as I followed the path on the right to the big pond. Ducks, gulls and moorhens drifted about.

Strolling beneath the willows, I came past the skateboard park and tennis courts on the left before bearing right, where they ended. A little beyond the corner of wetland, and the footbridge leading to the public library, was the big playing field.

Walking along the edge of it, I put Victoria Park behind me with a right turn onto the pavement of ultra-busy Torquay Road.

Soon I had passed Christ Church and Lower Polsham Road to take the pedestrian crossing for another right turn on the pavement by the big Jet garage. And there, in the high wall, was the gateway to Oldway Gardens.

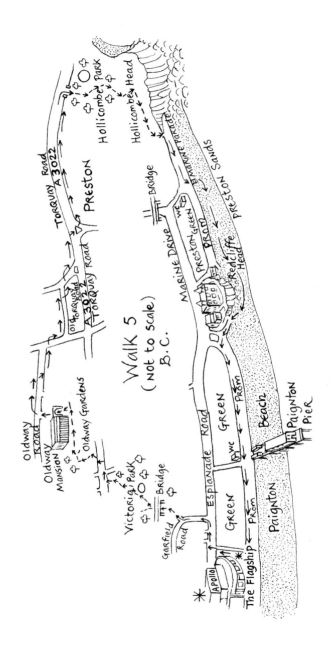

Walk 5
(not to scale)
B.C.

At the top of the narrow flight of steps it was left to the Grotto Gardens. Pines and palms stood above the rockery, and I idled past the mature horse chestnut tree for close-ups of the stream, the mini-ponds, rockery, and little waterfall. A gang of jackdaws were stalking an old lady who was dishing out bread to the waterbirds, pigeons, and grey squirrels.

Climbing the rough stone steps on the right, I came under the pines to the fork where I swung left past the rockery to be greeted by the delightful vision of cream and pale grey Oldway Mansion.

I walked the fine gravel path towards it with the lawns, mazelike miniature hedges, and flowerbeds on my left. Below, to the right, were the tennis courts. Swifts screamed high overhead, bees droned, and butterflies flickered in the heat ripple.

Wildlife cameos are a colourful aspect of the six acres of gardens, lawns, and woodland.

Then I was in the car park, coming left to look at the mansion's north facade.

Oldway is the Singer family's replica of the Palace of Versailles. Towards the end of the 19th century the American sewing-machine millionaire Isaac Merrit Singer brought his family to live in Paignton. But it was his son, Paris, a fan of French architecture, who was responsible, in 1904, for the mansion we see today. Every year thousands of visitors come to admire the north and east facades, with their huge pillars, beautiful balconies, and windows.

The affair between Paris and the dancer Isadora Duncan is well known, but few visitors are aware of the immortality achieved by his father's second wife, Isabella. The beautiful young French woman returned to France after her husband's death, and the sculptor Auguste Bartholdi persuaded her to model for him: the result was the Statue of Liberty.

The ground floor and first floors of the mansion are open to the public on Mondays to Fridays, 9 a.m. to 5 p.m.; Saturdays (summer), 9 a.m. to 5 p.m.; and Sundays (May to October), 2 p.m. to 5 p.m.

After a pleasant browse I came out the front door and turned left to walk through the giant arch and follow the path under the trees. Little Oldway was on the left. Birds called and the shadows were sun-dappled all the way to the gate at the end of the drive.

Author

Oldway Mansion, which was originally the home of the Singer family.

I crossed Oldway Road with the usual care, turned right, and walked down the pavement until a gap in the traffic gave me the chance to nip over to the other side. At the junction with Upper Manor Road I made another crossing in front of Oak Tree Garage. Then it was right again, with yesterday's sandstone farm buildings continuing left around the corner into Old Torquay Road.

Ye Olde Manor Fish Bar was on the right-hand side, and a bit further on I passed the Old Manor Inn.

It's a nostalgic trail for elderly locals, bringing ancestral things into focus. In this respect the word 'olde' does the trick.

At the crossroads I waited till it was safe to make it onto the pavement beside Preston Down Road. Then, just past Preston Baptist Church, I came up Torquay Road.

The nose-to-tail traffic was at a standstill. The traffic lights crossing was blocked by a navy blue Citroen, with five baseball-capped lads in it. Their heads were bobbing to the radio-blared rap.

The one in the passenger seat leaned out the window, glanced at my rucksack and trail boots, and said: 'You bloody stupid old git. Why walk in this heat when you can use your bus pass?'

His mates chuckled.

I shook my head, smiled, and said: 'Looking at you, son, I wish I had never gone to bed with your mother that night after drinking a gallon of lager'.

His mates hooted and whistled their appreciation of the reply, and I had crossed the road by the time the wag had recovered to put together some feeble blue abuse.

Relaxed, I loped up the Torquay Road pavement beyond the junction with Seaway Road, my ego inflated. I passed small shops, St Paul's Church, Living Waters Pentecostal Church, and the Shell garage at the top of the hill. Below, to the left, was the combe and its conifers – minus the gasometer. On my right was the row of dark, red sandstone cottages which were once the homes of the gasworks' employees.

The next downhill stretch brought me to the metal gates of Hollicombe Park which I entered, glad to get away from the traffic din, exhaust fumes, and baseball-capped cruds.

In the park ducks and moorhens were taking the sun beside the big pond. Herring gulls cackled from the lawns. Shrubs stirred feebly in a breeze that was like the draught from a hot oven.

Taking the path past the public toilets, which were closed, I side-stepped a meandering, scruffy-looking young bloke with greasy dreadlocks and carefully trimmed beard and moustache. Gazing at me like a demented goat, he defiantly tilted his can of Special Brew.

From the gate at the top of the park I came left over the little railway bridge and turned right onto Hollicombe Head for the familiar Bay views. House sparrow families hedge-hopped as they chirped.

The path and steps led to Preston's Marine Parade, with Paignton pier in the distance. There was a lot of prom activity and sunbathers chatted in deckchairs outside their beach huts. So I got a butterscotch ice cream from Marine Parade Refreshment Kiosk and went down the steps onto Preston Sands. The tide was out. If it hadn't been I could have used the raised path below the sea wall.

But it was fun to walk the damp, lower part of the beach, with the pier my target. Tourists were swimming, kids were paddling, and I crunched on below the headland where the Boathouse Restaurant, Redcliffe Hotel, and Villa Marina Luxury Hotel stand. Then I was on Paignton Beach which I abandoned to come along the seafront, beside the prom.

More families were having fun on the sands and North Green, and I was savouring the Bay and Channel views like I always do.

Walking along Bikini Boulevard I came under the pier. The public toilets were across the prom, opposite the pier steps. Kids could get donkey rides on the Green nearby, in the tradition of Donkey Daniels, that great local character of the old days.

The land train cruised by on its sedate journey along the prom; and four-wheeler buggy bikes were on the go. The ice cream and seafood kiosks were doing a roaring trade and I was confronted by a view of Paignton Harbour and Roundham Head. Speedboats and water-skiers were in top gear, yachts responded to the breeze, and senior citizens, with red faces and red arms and legs, dozed in deckchairs.

At the Flagship pub families were tucking into lunches in the smoke-free atmosphere. But I took my pint of draught Carlsberg Export onto the Sundeck, which is the rooftop beer garden.

The views raised the memories.

A couple enjoying a drink on the Sundeck.

Author

Well, with my sort of background, I'm not surprised that for most of my life I've been pub-oriented. My parents were spit-and-sawdust bards, preaching the 'Gospel of the Bottle and the Barrel'. Their enthusiasm for good, wholesome beers was infectious. Weekend pub regulars, they didn't hurry down their ale with a reckless boozer's disregard for the subtleties of individual brews and flavours.

Where beer was concerned they had refined tastes and I've followed in their footsteps, with a preference for blond beer and real ale.

No wonder I'm a fan of *Inn Outings*.

6. High on the Haldons Trail

Start and finish point: Bishopsteignton – The Ring of Bells pub (SX 910 737).
Distance: About 4 miles.
Degree of difficulty: Grade C.
Route: The Ring of Bells pub; Rowden Cross; Gypsy Corner; Little Haldon Cross; Old Walls Hill; Radway Hill; and back to the pub.

It was Sunday morning. House martins flew low through the spring sunshine over Bishopsteignton where my 'chauffeur' had dropped me off at the Ring of Bells, the old pub at the junction of Radway Hill and Fore Street.

The Ring of Bells, Bishopsteignton.

Chris Carter

Before setting off I had a glance through a very worn volume of *The Open Road*, 'a little book for the Wayfarer', compiled by E. V. Lucas, and published for the first time in 1899. My copy is the 15th Methuen Edition which came out in 1909.

Slotting the book back into my lightweight rucksack, I walked along the raised pavement of Fore Street. On the roof of the cottage called Cloche Merle, which was once the local plague house, a blackbird was in full song. Then it was interesting houses all the way up and beyond The Pasty Mine, where some of my favourite pasties are made.

A lot of historic buildings are at the centre of Bishopsteignton, and I was passing the war memorial and Methodist Church, with the village hall over the road. At the fork I turned right to come up Clanage Street, for a close-up of another village pub, the Bishop John de Grandisson, before climbing steep Smith Hill, which took me out of Bishopsteignton. Sunlight between clouds gave the countryside a wonderful clarity, and there was a fine view of the Teign from Murley Crescent.

At Clanage Cross another right turn sent me on my way up Lindridge Hill, with Haldon and Exeter on the signpost. But first of all I paused to take in more of those Teign valley views, where the estuary swept down to Shaldon and the dark headland called The Ness.

A cock chaffinch flitted about in the hedge. The road was narrow and the hedgebanks covered in ferns, alexanders, cow parsley, and other umbellifers. At the cemetery, on the bend, I took a breather to look upriver towards Newton Abbot and Dartmoor. From the brow of the hill there was another field-patched landscape. A lady, walking a couple of Jack Russells, gave me a friendly smile as we exchanged 'good mornings', and a few cars passed, reminding me that this was a route along country roads.

'ER'S SCRUMPY-puggled OR mezzed as a brish'

Farmland rolled to the foothills of the moors, and on the far horizon were familiar tors. That view is one of the many bonuses of this hilly little hike.

Then I was at Rowden Cross for the right turn, signposted: 'Haldon and Exeter'. Coming up the hill, I met a car driven by a young mother, with her two children on the back seat. The little girl poked her tongue out at me, and the little boy grinned like Tarzan's chimp.

Ambushed by another rural panorama of low hills and combes, backed by Dartmoor's in-country, I continued the long hill climb. On the right, at the next bend, a lane led to Higher Radway Farm. Gorse was in flower at the gate, and the small, round, waxy-green leaves of pennywort showed amongst the hedgebank ferns and flowers.

Nature's small-print tells me a lot. But the calm of Humber Down Wood was shattered by the manic screeching of a jay. I was between woodland where mature beeches created a cathedral nave atmosphere. The walking was ever upward, which is a novelty for me after a lifetime of going mainly downhill!

On the right, near the top, was the wood used by scrambler bike enthusiasts.

At Gypsy Corner I ignored the right-hand turn and came on to walk the grass verge, beside Teignmouth Golf Course, to Little Haldon Cross at the top of the hill. From the pebble-and-gravel car park I could look over the heather, brambles and gorse, and miles of farmland, with the vision of Dartmoor crowned with Rippon Tor, Saddle Tor, and Hay Tor, on the blue horizon.

Cloud shadows swept across the landscape, and it would have been difficult to imagine a more glorious countryside under such a vast sky. It was the kind of beauty Cotman enshrined in his watercolour paintings. But only classical music can capture the essence of this sort of magic. On that occasion, though, the birdsong was enough.

Meanwhile, the sun on new leaves, grasses, and flowers was part of May's appeal. No wonder it's my favourite month, with October a close second.

At Little Haldon Cross all I needed was the countryside, the sky, cloud shadows, and solitude that held the scents of the season.

One of the extensive views from Little Haldon.

Chris Carter

But the beauty of the place and the casual nature study were paving the way to the lunchtime pub. Called to the bar, I knew that around noon I would be enjoying the company of a frisky, Danish blonde back at the Ring of Bells.

Retracing my steps to Gypsy Corner, I turned left and continued alongside the golf course. A shower fell but soon passed. The sun was even brighter when it shone again. Columns of rain drifted across Lyme Bay as another view opened up ahead.

At the entrance to the golf clubhouse I swung right to begin the next stage of the circuit at Little Haldon Heath. Striding on, I came down Old Walls Hill, past Shepherds' Lane over on the left. Between the hedgerow trees was yet another great view of Shaldon and The Ness.

The descent was steep. I could see Teignmouth's suburbs below the coastal pastures. Beyond the popular seaside town the Channel gleamed all the way to the cloudy horizon.

Soon I was looking at the small, ancient fields on the outskirts of Bishopsteignton. Their high, wild hedges are a V-sign in the face of intensive farming.

The narrow country road ran down to the levels and around

the corner by the remains of the Bishops' Palace, known as Old Walls. Originally it was a Benedictine monastery. But when the monks pulled out in the 11th century, the bishops of Exeter claimed it as their summer palace – a kind of ecclesiastical holiday home.

The road brought me past the row of tall, hedgerow poplars called The Twelve Apostles; and near the junction with Radway Street was some handsome modern housing. But I prefer the farm that was there not so long ago.

Never mind. I was back in Bishopsteignton, turning right at Whidborne Manor. Bronescombe Avenue was on the left and a moment later I stopped to have a look at the Old Forge housing development, where that great village character, Dicky Bird, is recalled on a little bird-shaped plaque over the garage door.

Walking on, I passed historic, black and white Radway House for the left turn onto Radway Hill. Over the rooftops was a memorable view of the Teign estuary hills.

The old almshouses provided the final architectural flourish, and there I was, back at the Ring of Bells. Across the road, at the top of Shute Hill, was the community centre that had once been the village school. The 12th century parish church was just down the road.

The Cask Marque plaque outside the pub door stated: 'This house serves quality cask beers'. A moment later I was in the small bar, with its low wooden ceiling and traditional lighting. It had a pool table, dartboard, and fireplace. A couple of big beer barrels, with flat tops, had been converted into side tables, complete with stools.

Down two or three steps was the neat restaurant. The pub was once a beer house, and the restaurant area was the old bar.

On my visit the Ring of Bells had various real ales, a choice of wines, some fine whiskies and other spirits; cider, the cask beers, half a dozen good lagers and a tempting menu. But I was more than happy to stand at the bar with my Danish blonde, which was, of course, a pint of frisky Carlsberg Export lager.

That, and a bowl of home-made mushroom soup, with a roll and butter, was enough for me.

7. The Lighthouse and Lyte House Circuit

Start and finish point: Brixham – Berry Head Visitor Centre (SX 944 565).

Distance: About $3^{1}/_{2}$ miles.

Degree of difficulty: Grade A.

Route: Berry Head Visitor Centre; Gillard Road and Rea Barn Road; Mudstone Lane; Durl Head; Berry Head South Fort and North Fort; the lighthouse; the Berry Head Hotel; and back to the Visitor Centre.

From Berry Head Visitor Centre I left the car park and came up Gillard Road. Very few cars were about. It was 11 o'clock in the morning at the end of February, and South Devon had been enjoying a week of dry, cold, sunny weather. A sea mist was lifting off the Channel.

In fleece, tracksuit trousers, and strong boots I walked past the holiday camp chalets and the old hedge of ash, blackthorn, and hazel. Blackthorn blossom drifted down into the wayside nettles and ferns. On the left were the remaining meadows of an ancient field system.

Then Sea Lane was behind me and I was striding along Rea Barn Road, wary of anything on four wheels. Far too often I've seen relatives of the Grim Reaper in the driving seat of cars going too fast.

I was glad to turn left into Mudstone Lane which brought me onto the South West Coast Path, which was signposted. Another left turn and I came over the stile above St Mary's Bay. A wren blasted me with his loud territorial song, a greenfinch twittered a reply, and a couple of backpackers, cock and hen, hurried by, stern and silent.

Continuing my up-and-down nature trail, I was grateful for the firm, dry walking conditions. Clifftop scrub and the sea were on the right, and the mess of pigeons' feathers on the path was the result of a fox kill. Sparrowhawks leave a neat 'puddle' of feathers, whereas foxes are far less fussy.

While passing a clump of alexanders I saw a comma butterfly among the blackthorn blossom, before I left another stile in my wake to come across the sloping meadow on the edge of the cliffs. Rabbits legged it into the brambles.

The path ran on between thorn thickets, with fulmar cackle in the background. The musk of fox was briefly on the air. It smelled like cats' piddle. Used to it, I went over the stiles, field by field, to Durl Head where I looked back at the bulk of South Down and the headlands beyond. Then another stile saw me into the final meadow, which is bright with wildflowers in the late spring and summer. They include the delicate, pink, common centaury.

Leaving the meadow at the last stile, I climbed the turf slope to the ramparts of the South Fort (the Old Redoubt) and its dry moat.

From mid-April to August this clifftop grassland has a marvellous display of the very rare white rock roses. On my winter trail, though, I was pleased to see primroses, bugle, fennel, and the tiny white flowers of barren strawberry.

Walking left, between the hawthorn copse and the moat, I was back at Berry Head Visitor Centre, with the best part of the circuit to come.

From the top of the car park I came along the footpath listening to the herring gulls. Those 'Brixham bagpipes' were warming up for a day of wailing, moaning, and cackling. For obvious reasons Torbay locals call them 'shite hawks'!

The path took me beside the common to the entrance of the North Fort, which, like the Old Redoubt, was built during the Napoleonic Wars. The North Fort battery of guns protected the Channel fleet which often anchored in Tor Bay.

And there was the Bay on my left. People were out and about, and I was mulling over the various attractions of the National Nature Reserve (NNR), which is managed by Torbay Coast and Countryside Trust.

Berry Head is a great limestone 'mausoleum', packed with the remains of distant geological ages. The rock is composed of the compressed shells of molluscs and crustaceons. It has a pale luminosity.

Thousands of seabirds breed on the cliffs; and, in season, over 500 species of wildflowers grow throughout the Country Park. Among the botanical rarities are the white rock roses, goldilocks aster, small hare's-ear, small rest-harrow, carrot broomrape, and honeywort.

Throughout the year the NNR has a lot to offer, from migrant birds and butterflies, to the resident wildlife which includes foxes, bats, badgers, rabbits; adders, grass snakes, slow-worms, and common lizards. Recent introductions were the three or four feral goats, which are usually hidden in the clifftop scrub, where they feed. Among the seabirds are shags, cormorants, kittiwakes, fulmars, gulls, and the biggest colony of common guillemots on the south coast. In early spring guillemots can be seen at their ceremonial courtship dance on the water at the base of the cliffs.

Passing the North Fort Cafe, I strolled on to the tip of the headland. On the left were the coastguard station, and the lighthouse which is the highest and lowest in the UK. How come? Well, the building is only about 15 feet tall, but the clifftop where it stands is 200 feet above the sea.

Again the Bay views were remarkable, with the hills of Torquay emerging from the mist as it continued to thin. Inland were Dartmoor's hills, and it was that mariner's vision of the skyline tors that gave the Bay its name.

Retracing my steps, I swung right beyond the North Fort and came down the footpath through the trees below the common. Screened by the bare branches and the conifers, the Berry Head Hotel was on the clifftop, facing the Bay. Here and there I found evidence of badger digging. Then I left the trees at the bottom of the path for the right turn along the narrow road. A few yards later it was sharp right into the grounds of the hotel, which is in my Top Ten Torbay buildings.

After making sure my boots were really clean I went in. But before settling at a table in the Lyte Bar I had a look at the Lyte Bar Terrace.

The panoramic view of Tor Bay and Lyme Bay is enough to have you reaching for the champagne. To the north were

The Berry Head Hotel, which dates back to 1809.
Courtesy of the Berry Head Hotel

Torquay's hills. Eastward was the misty Channel. A Brixham trawler headed out to sea.

In the bar it was difficult to believe the hotel was built in 1809 as a military hospital for the garrison of the Berry Head forts. When the troops departed, after the defeat of Napoleon, the hospital was left empty. But in 1833 it became the home of the Reverend Henry Francis Lyte, the vicar of All Saints Church, Brixham. He wrote the words of 'Abide with me', one of the best-loved hymns in the English language.

Terminally ill with TB, in 1847, he would have watched the sun go down behind Dartmoor's hills, only to appear again on the Bay horizon at daybreak.

The clergyman died that year in the south of France, but lives on in his hymn, which echoes the parable of death and resurrection that is sunset and sunrise.

It was pleasant to admire the bar decor. The oak-beamed ceiling was low, the log-effect fire very convincing, and the views from the windows couldn't have been better. The emphasis is on comfort, in a relaxed atmosphere.

There were plenty of beers on draught and a couple of real ales. I liked the Breakfast Menu headings – Mate's Breakfast (from nautical terminology, not blokes' bar talk) and Skipper's Breakfast. The wide variety of top quality food is delightful.

Munching my roast beef and horseradish sandwich, I recalled other visits to the hotel, and some of the Lyte Bar Terrace Bay wildlife cabarets. The owner told me about several sightings of bottle-nosed dolphins, and the grey seal that was a regular visitor to the rocks at the foot of the local cliff.

Slightly more famous visitors and guests include David Essex, John Cleese, Rick Parfitt of Status Quo; Adam Ant, and Lord Callaghan. But local legend also claims that Napoleon was often brought ashore here, as a prisoner off a British warship anchored in the Bay. He spent a few evenings in the house where he had an affair with a young lady: the result was a baby boy.

But standing at one of the bar windows, with a glass of real ale, and winter drawing to a close, it was the Lyte connection that came to mind. I watched distances firming while the last of the mist vanished and Torbay's three towns caught the sun.

After that short but pleasant break I came up narrow Berry Head Road, past the wood, Berry Head Cottages, and what was once Berry Head Farm, and the common, to the NNR car park where my son arrived to drive me home.

✳ ✳ ✳ ✳ ✳

8. The Merry Mycologists' Trail

Start and finish point: Marldon – The Church House Inn (SX 866 636).
Distance: About 6 miles.
Degree of difficulty: Grade C.
Route: The Church House Inn; Marldon Cross; Westerland Lane; Cruel Cross; Westerland valley; Buttshill Cross; Cruel Cross; Marldon Cross; and back to the pub.

I was in Marldon, the village on the edge of Torbay. The name comes from Mergheldone ('Hill where gentian grows'): in Old English it was Meargealla-dun. Gentian is a blue- or violet-coloured, trumpet-shaped flower. There are 17 varieties in the UK and northern Europe, but I don't know which one was common in the Marldon countryside.

That fine October morning, though, I was thinking of other things as I left the Church House Inn. Behind the public car park was Jubilee Meadow, the community field where Marldon Apple Pie Fair attracts thousands of visitors every year, on the last Saturday in July.

Above the white front of the inn, with its black paintwork, I could see the tower of the Church of St John the Baptist. Wood pigeons crooned and I was walking up Village Road, beyond the church steps, past Rock Cottage, Fernley Cottage, and Smithy Cottage, on the right, and Vine Cottage on the left.

It was all uphill by Pottery Mews and Old Greystone Barn to Marldon Cross Hill, and left opposite Kiln Road. Soon I was passing Marldon Grove and Moor Tor Manor. The parade of bungalows and their gardens saw me past the primary school, with more bungalows, as well as some tall hedges on each side of the road.

Not far from the village shops and post office, Marldon Cross was waiting. And after nipping across the busy back road, which was once the main route to Totnes, I turned right and walked the pavement beneath the hawthorn hedge, with its deep red haws.

Then I came left into Westerland Lane, which saw me under the hazel bushes, through drifts of fallen leaves, to Middle Westerland House.

Although I was on a narrow, winding road, that led to isolated properties, it was really an updated country lane trail through a classic Devon valley. The tall, wild hedges, lack of traffic, and the sunset colours of the local farmland, emphasised this. I glanced

The joys of the country road.

Author

over my shoulder, expecting to see the ghosts of fellow rural romantics, like George Trevelyan, E. M. Smyth, Edward Thomas, Edward Bowen, and E. V. Lucas, following me. Not a soul. But there was a lot of movement in the sky, with flocks of songbirds doing the rounds.

At the bend I turned left into a wider lane, past an old barn, a new barn, a few cider apple trees, and a property called Little Westerland. The wayside hazels had littered the surface with leaves and nuts, and grey squirrels were cashing in: for the ever-alert 'shadow tails' October is 'Bonanza Month', with its harvests of hazelnuts, beechmast, acorns, and berries.

Westerland valley is home to a lot of wildlife, with its ancient woodland, hedges and grassland. Passing the Old Farmhouse, I loved the seasonal colours glowing around me. The leaves of cranesbill were a brighter red than those of the brambles. Peacock, red admiral, and tortoiseshell butterflies fluttered about in the sun.

At Cruel Cross I turned right, with a low hedge on one side and a high, wild one on the other. While I walked I weighed up the satisfaction nature study has given me over the years, from the wildflowers in jam jars on the primary school classroom table, to mammalogy and in-depth study of foxes, badgers, and otters in my teens. That gave me a firm foundation for three of my animal novels.

Well, peace of mind is high on the list of rewards that can come from lane walking.

The warm colours of the trees had been heightened by early frosts. 'Bullens' covered the blackthorn bushes. Bracken was fox-coloured, fading to dull yellow at the tips, and many of the hedges were hung with old man's beard.

Soon I was at the stream that flows first on one side, then the other side of the lane. On the bark of the two nearby oaks was the knobbly, black, King Alfred's Cakes fungus.

The lane wound on and up … and up, for a long way, into mist-smudged distances. I followed it, while flocks of wood pigeons, finches, and starlings blotted the landscape. Then I met a gang of cheerfully intense 'twitchers'.

'Seen any cirls?' one asked.

'No', I grinned. 'But a couple of earwigs were lap-dancing at Cruel Cross. And by the way, lads, you would be wise to put on your helmets. The local woodpeckers are very busy at this time of year.'

They glanced nervously at each other, smiled at me, nodded, and departed at a slightly quicker pace, while I enjoyed the sight of the ancient woodland called Ramshill Copse. It was on the hillside to the right, above the gorse thickets.

Fortunately the local hedges hadn't been 'well-groomed'. I share the cirl buntings' preference for bushy field hedges like those on the low hill to the left. Somebody was wandering above the shallow combe, and I hoped it was a mycologist on one of those erratic mushroom trails I used to take through childhood autumns with my mother.

Among my favourite edible fungi are oyster mushroom, field, shaggy cap, morel, parasol, grisette, and brown wood.

Sheep bleated as rooks joined them on the top pastures, pigeons clattered into the nameless copse on the left side of the valley, and a few money spiders drifted by on strands of gossamer thread, off on long or short migration flights.

Less daintily I climbed to Buttshill Cross and looked back into the valley. Sunlight had strengthened and colour flared on trees and hedges.

A sharp left turn brought me above Higher Blagdon, and soon I had a gateway view across farmland to the hills of the South Hams.

Walking on, I knew there were circles of fairy ring toadstools, several species of edible boletus mushrooms and wood-blewit toadstools, nearby; and honey tuft fungus on fallen timber and tree stumps.

Passing a cowhouse, I could look over the low hedges into the red soil autumn views before I came left at the crossroads and saw the traffic on the main road where the valley ended.

Rats, scuttling about in the hedge bottom, roused my curiosity, and among the brambles I saw a plastic lavatory seat.

The Church House Inn, Marldon.

Chris Carter

Despite my contempt for fly-tipper vandals, that use the countryside as a dump, I must admit the abandoned loo seat, framing bramble leaves, gave me an idea for my Tate Gallery Turner Prize entry.

Before long I was back beyond Cruel Cross, reversing my route uphill to Westerland Lane and Marldon Cross. Then the walk downhill brought me to the Church House Inn, which dates from 1362.

Logs blazed in the stovelike fireplace near the main door, highlighting that part of the public bar, with its low ceiling and flagstone floor. The logs needed no encouragement to create a welcome glow. Flame reflections flickered on the low ceiling and oak beams above the wooden furniture.

At the bar I was told about the six cask beers, the four real ales, the lagers, cider, half a dozen malt whiskies, wines, and champagne by the glass.

Then there was the skittle alley, and near the main restaurant the tiny nook restaurant had once been the village bakery. One of the barmaids referred to it as the 'Oven Room'. The wide variety of food is top quality, and the inn's atmosphere warm and friendly. No wonder the Church House is included in Egon Ronay's *2006 Guide to the Best Restaurants and Gastropubs in the UK*.

For pub-buffs like me the bar is very much part of the rural idyll, which has to include an inn, church, village green, thatched cottages, and yesterday's farms.

But sentimental romance apart, a good pub fire always helps me relax over a pint of real ale – with a large dash of nostalgia.

9. The Totnes – Withy Pond Trail

Start and finish point: Totnes – The Steam Packet Inn (SX 806 599).
Distance: About $3^1/2$ miles.
Degree of difficulty: Grade B.
Route: The Steam Packet Inn; the Totnes to Ashprington Cycle and Footpath; Sharpham Estate; Linhay Plantation; Withy Pond; and back to the Steam Packet Inn.

It was a cold, frosty, and sunny December morning, and I was in Little Totnes, an historic part of the town. The Steam Packet is on Saint Peter's Quay, beside the tidal Dart. The handsome old hostelry was built in 1740 and remained the New London Inn until 1850 when the name was changed.

Leaving the pub at the end of New Walk, I came sharp right up Moat Hill for a few yards before the left turn onto the hard-

The author stood in the doorway of the Steam Packet Inn.
Chris Carter

surfaced Totnes to Ashprington Cycle and Footpath, which is clearly signposted.

The posh lane took me up above the fields and the estuary. A tall, naked hedge was on the right. Saint Peter's Quay and Baltic Wharf were down below to the left, with Bridgetown on the far hillside above the river. Where the houses ended, the farmland began.

From the hill climb I could look back at Totnes, Totnes Bridge, and Brutus Bridge, as the lane wound on. Then there were great estuary views from the top of a low wall.

Passing cyclists were usually considerate. I didn't need signposts or a map. The path was my guide – or is this the Irish in me speaking?

Grey squirrels were busy in the wood on the left. The notice on the gate at the top of the hill read: 'Dogs on lead. Livestock'. Then

A section of the Totnes to Ashprington Cycle and Footpath.
Chris Carter

I was walking a broad ride and looking down into classic views of the countryside. The landscape, with its silvery sheen, was beautiful under a blue sky.

Loitering with content, I watched flights of duck and wild geese splashing down. Cattle meditated beneath a beech tree on the hillside, and the cow dung on the path was frost-hardened.

Beyond the gate, signed Sharpham, I found myself high above the river, looking down on the narrows called Home Reach. The next gate also presented attractive views, and I was remembering visits to Sharpham Vineyard.

A moment later a gang of top-hatted herons skipped past, maybe heading for a binge at Totnes. Sheep huddled together beneath the trees were chuckling. But soon I was savouring the view of the salt marshes beside the estuary, and going past another gate carrying a 'Livestock – Dogs' warning.

Passing Linhay Plantation, I noted the ruins of the barns on the hillside across the river. More wildfowl were on the wing and I was above the salt marshes, with the houses of Sharpham Barton on the hillside to my right. The signpost, near the bridge over the stream, marked the meeting place of the paths. On the right was little Withy Pond and its mini-boardwalk. Withy is the branch of a willow used mainly in basket-making.

The pond was my turning point. It's popular with school groups on nature trails; and natural history is one of the main attractions of this hike.

A casual browse around the pond, and a binocular vision of shelduck flying upstream from their breeding site at Bow Creek, set the seal on my walk. Britain's largest duck, the shelduck adults were back after their moulting migration to Heligoland Bight. And I was happy to retrace my steps for the new river views and the prospect of a blond beer at the end of the hike.

Moving at a brisk pace, I soon reached the Steam Packet Inn. Above the bar doorway, beyond the foyer, the little notice told me to 'Duck or Grouse'. Being tall, I'm glad I took the advice!

The Christmas decorations were a colourful part of the festive season atmosphere, and the low lighting included candles in bottles on the tables.

There was a selection of fine wines and malt whiskies. Real ales were on tap, alongside the bitters. But it was the Kronenbourg draught lager that caught my eye.

The good food ranges from the à la carte menu and daily specials, to the bar snacks. Wherever possible local produce is used. Gourmets won't be disappointed.

From the window near the restaurant I could see the terrace beer garden, overlooking the river. Steamer Quay was across the water and Vire Island a few yards upstream.

Then, with a pint of Kronenbourg, I planted myself on one of the comfortable leather settees by the fire, hoping my lift wouldn't arrive too soon.

Note: The Steam Packet car park is for customers only. If you are doing the walk park elsewhere, like the pay-and-display car park off St Katharine's Way; and clean your boots before entering the pub.

✳ ✳ ✳ ✳ ✳

10. The Torcorn Hill Circuit

Start and finish point: Woolston Green – The Live & Let Live Inn
(SX 778 660).
Distance: About 4 miles.
Degree of difficulty: Grade B.
Route: The Live & Let Live Inn; Gullaford; Halswell; Forder
Green; Waytown; Sparkwell Cross; and the pub again.

The December morning was grey and misty when I left the Live &
Let Live Inn at Woolston Green and headed towards Landscove. I
was glad to have the freedom of the quiet country roads to walk
the Torcorn Hill circuit. The 460-feet hill is central to the whole
route. A well-known local landmark, it's covered in small fields,
with a copse or two.

I was in cagoule, tracksuit trousers, and the leather walking
boots. There's nothing demanding about the trail, nothing to
excite hikers interested only in distance. Four miles? That's just an
old dear's pre-breakfast stroll, mate. And that's what many
mature walkers go for, most of them on a regular basis.

A big flock of starlings settled in the trees as I took the first
right-hand turn just beyond the pub, where the narrow road was
no more than a lane. But it was a busy corner of rural South
Devon, with a lot of farming activity in the fields.

Winter wheat was among the grassland, cattle were in the
nearby pasture, and the surface of the lane was mud-glossed. On
the right, at the end of the private lane, was Blackler Farm, with
Torcorn ghostly in the background. The mix of agricultural smells
got up my nose, and I grinned, recalling my mother's response to
the pong, which she called 'scarecrow's aftershave'.

There was a big pond in the combe to the right, and a crow
rasped at me as I walked past the cider apple orchard and flail-
mowed hedges to Gullaford Cross and the farm. Yes, it was
clockwise all the way, while a dog barked from a bungalow
garden and a cock pheasant hiccuped like Dad when he was
pigging a full English breakfast.

A bit further on I crossed the River Hems, which is just a little stream. River? OK, in that case Danny De Vito is Goliath and my fluffy little, long-haired, black and white she cat, Scruffy, is the Beast of Brixham.

Then it was uphill and down, with the landscape still mist-blurred. Moments later I was turning right at the T-junction, the way signposted Broadhempston, to walk up the narrow road past Wayford Cottage.

Mysterious agricultural goings-on brought a touch of drama to the countryside. I was happy to be among working farms like Halswell, with its barns, outhouses, and muddy yard. But the giant pylon behind, with cables crackling like mad, lent the morning a definite sci-fi touch.

Starlings everywhere were in good voice. Then they joined the

confusion of rooks and wood pigeons scattering as the shooting began. The crack and bang of twelve-bores sent the rooks flapping away across the bare trees, and I was glad to be gravity-bound to the muddy road, en route to Younghouse and another busy farm. On my right were three old, weathered-stone cottages, and the yellow walls of a big house.

Barns were on both sides of the road, and the cattle in the field corner stared at me. The message was: 'watch it – a townie alien is sussing out the scene. Him have look of beef-eater.'

Passing Forder House, at Forder Green, I noted the ferny hedgebanks while the shooting continued to punctuate the starling cries.

It wasn't long before I reached Waytown Cross to come to the right along the narrow road, downhill past more banks glossy with harts tongue ferns. I hadn't met a car or a fellow wayfarer. But I wasn't complaining. Solitude is great - in small doses.

Waytown, of course, isn't a town. It's a handful of cottages and houses at the roadside.

At the fork I turned right. Barns could be seen over the wall, and against the top hedge of the field, on the left, sheep were penned, and poultry were in their runs next door. Three magpies swayed on the wall, like priests high on magic mushrooms.

For me it was up, then down, and back against the hedge to let a tractor and trailer rumble by. Geese were sounding off, ducks quacked, and cocks crowed.

The winding lane took me past a field full of what looked like wrecked cars, and I was leaving Bickaton Farm behind. Torcorn Hill was close by, there on the right, half-hidden in the mist. A collie barked, and beyond the old farmhouse was a yard full of tractors. More cattle watched me through the bars of a gate, and a few primroses showed on the hedgebanks.

The view from along part of a winding lane.

Author

After Beaston the River Hems was suddenly on the left, beside the road. And soon I was crossing it at Port Bridge. From Portbridge Cross it was straight on, signposted: 'Staverton and Buckfastleigh'. Sparkwell was to the left.

OK, Hems is just a brook, but that's part of its appeal. In any case our ancestors were entitled to their excursions into mythology. Maybe a surfeit of mead was responsible. God knows what I would have called the Hems after half a dozen pints of premium lager and a few double whiskies.

Walking uphill towards Sparkwell Cross, I had close-ups of raindrops on bramble twigs. Winter wheat had that flush of artificial-looking green about it, and glancing over my shoulder I saw Torcorn Hill emerging from the mist. But not for long.

A few cars met and passed each other with difficulty, a pair of jackdaws jangled, and a big tractor went by. At Sparkwell Cross I swung right and came up the fairly busy, wider road under those crackling cables. An old orchard was on the right, and presently I was loping past Woolston Green Methodist Church to the Live & Let Live Inn.

Unlike Ray Mears, on one of his TV *Extreme Survival* jaunts, I wasn't dreaming of a mouth-watering, nutritious larvae meal. I was looking forward to a bar snack.

The pleasant 19th century inn has various real ales on tap, lagers, wines, and whiskies. And it was good to find the open fire warming the bar where customers can get lunch or an evening meal. The food ranges from tasty starters, main meals, daily specials, and the Sunday Roast.

It was a typical Devon village pub, with its window alcoves and cheerful regulars on the bar stools. The car park and Orchard Beer Garden were across the road.

My sausages and chips snack and a pint of Bass were all the refreshment I required. But I was ready for another pint when my son ambled in, jangling the car keys. Naturally, it was on the lad.

The Live & Let Live Inn, Woolston Green.
Courtesy of the Live & Let Live Inn

11. The Cockington Country Park Trail

Start and finish point: Cockington – Pay-and-display car park (SX 893 637).
Distance: About 3 miles.
Degree of difficulty: Grade A.
Route: The pay-and-display car park, Cockington Village; the meadows footpath; Cockington Lane; the lakes; Gamekeeper's Cottage; Warren Barn; the stone cider press; the drive; Cockington Court Craft Centre; the stables and gardens; and the Drum Inn.

I began in the centre of Cockington Village on a warm, windy June morning. The pay-and-display car park was just up the road, not far from the Drum Inn.

Every roof around the centre is thatched. Nesting swallows dipped in and out of The Forge, which is 500 years old. The other buildings nearby were The Old Granary Gift Shop, Weavers Cottage Tea Rooms, The Old School House Gift Shop, and Rose Cottage. A couple of the famous horse-drawn carriages were parked in the village square ready to take visitors on a scenic trip to Cockington Court.

After a brief browse I was off down Cockington Lane. A couple of ducks dozed on the roof of Rose Cottage. Below them were the lawns, rockeries, fish pond, apple orchard, and raised tea garden terrace beneath its green canopy. Mallard dozed under the apple trees. The pianist was playing and customers were eating and drinking in the tea garden.

I walked past yesterday's farms and today's conversions which were once barns, stables, or cowsheds. The stream was on the left, beside the narrow road which is Cockington Lane. A huge horse chestnut tree towered over the garden of Lanscombe Lodge Cottage.

Striding along below the hedge, I came to the Cockington hawthorn that blossoms in the spring and at Christmas. A blackbird was singing as I passed Lanscombe House Hotel tea

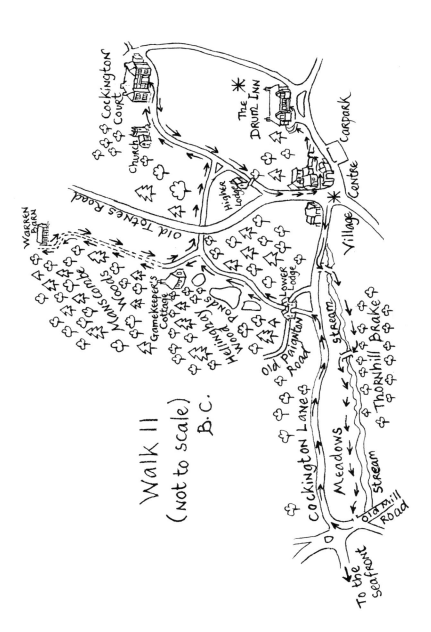

Walk 11
(not to scale)
B.C.

gardens and came through the gate on the left onto the public footpath that runs through the valley water-meadows.

Half a dozen vintage tourists from the Midlands were laughing and joking beside the stream. Meanwhile, the path brought me into a late spring vision of wildflowers and elder blossom. Leaves had lost their May radiance, but the gradual deepening of greens was soothing.

The yellow flags and marsh marigolds by the stream echoed the gold of the meadow buttercups. A chiffchaff nagged away and the dusty path, which is wheelchair and pushchair friendly, followed the stream.

Where the valley became wider I crossed a stone footbridge onto the boardwalk above the wetland. Thornhill Brake was to the left. At dawn and dusk, on a few occasions, I've seen roe-deer on the edge of this sloping wood.

The walking was pleasant and I was glad to find so many family groups taking advantage of the Country Park and the weather.

Soon the boards gave way to a hard-surfaced footpath. Down beside the stream ash and willow fidgeted in the breeze. Then I was at the end of the water-meadows, going through the gate that saw me onto Old Mill Road. A sharp right turn, round the bend, brought me into Cockington Lane, ever-wary of traffic. (**Note:** If you have young children with you it would be wise to retrace your steps along the valley path, and leave it at the gate to bear left, then right, to go up the narrow road that brings you under the arch of Lower Lodge to the lakes.)

The hedgebanks, each side of the lane, were one of those botanical shows that fascinate me, season after season. And, for amateur nature detectives, there were also conspicuous badger and fox runs.

I was walking through one of those 'tunnels of green gloom' poets love. Snatches of birdsong, and sunlight gleaming on ivy leaves, spiced the experience. But it was the green alkanet, stitchwort, red campion, bluebells, and harts tongue ferns that caught my eye.

A horse-drawn carriage passed, en route to the railway bridge near the seafront. Malcolm, the driver, slowed the horses, grinned, turned to his four passengers, and said: 'That's Brian, the village idiot'.

'Well, with a father like you what d'you expect?' I replied, and the passengers laughed.

Moments later I was turning left under the giant ash onto the narrow road that was signposted: 'Gamekeeper's Cottage, The Lakes, and Woodland Walk'.

It saw me up and under the arch of Lower Lodge, past the rhododendron thickets to the first of the three lakes, which my generation would call ponds. So, I'll show my age and do just that. A solitary moorhen was on the bottom one and plenty of gunnera, or 'elephant ear rhubarb', as I call it, could be seen under the trees of Hellinghay Wood.

At the carp pond big, ghostly fish were gliding about in the brown water which is the ideal habitat for that species. A white duck sat on a tree stump and waggled her butt like one of the Cheeky Girls. The path narrowed and I stopped to look at the foxgloves among the nettles before strolling to the top pond, where the murky brown surface played host to just one drake. Maybe he was the godfather of the Cockington Mallard Mafia.

Turning left, I followed the path to the Gamekeeper's Cottage. Burnt down in 1990, it was restored and is now an educational centre for day visits by schools.

Leaving the cottage, the path brought me to the right into Manscombe Wood and along the dusty red track above the combe. According to some authorities Man, in the wood's name, is a reference to the Saxon word for evil. So Manscombe is 'the evil valley'. But I believe a more likely derivation is Maen, the Celtic word for stone. Stony Valley probably has the equivalent in Mansands, the pebbly beach south of Berry Head.

Opposite the woodland bank a little stream trickled beside a stone wall, and before long I was at the ruins of Warren Barn. The old building would soon have a complete facelift to become a residential, outdoor education centre for schools. Like all these sort of projects, within the Country Park, the driving force was Torbay Coast and Countryside Trust.

Turning, I made my way back to the Gamekeeper's Cottage and the top pond. The footpaths are well signposted.

Coming up the narrow road, which is used by the horse-drawn carriages, I passed the high, vertical, red mud banks. On the far side of the arch of the bridge carrying the old Totnes Road I stood beneath one of the mature oaks, which are features of the Country Park. Then I was swinging left at the big, round, stone cider press, and the grass triangle dominated by a handsome conifer.

This evergreen is the deodar, the sacred tree of the Indians. On home territory it grows on the lower slopes of the Himalayas.

Walking on, I came past the mature limes beside the drive leading to Cockington Court. At the top of the grassy slopes, on the left, were the Arboretum, Dew Park, and Lady's Park, where each spring there's a fine display of the pale lilac-coloured flowers called Ladies' Smocks.

A lot of people were about and the cricket field, in the broad combe, was catching the sun. Then I was below the wildflower bank of the Church of St George and St Mary.

It was noon and none of the tables outside the cafe at Cockington Court were empty. The historic building was owned by the Carys in the 14th century and acquired by the Mallock family in 1654. Torquay Borough Council bought it in 1933, and today it is a craft centre and the HQ of Torbay Coast and Countryside Trust, which is responsible for the environment-friendly management of the Country Park and almost all Torbay's green places.

After visiting the craft shops I went round the back to the Rose Garden, Stable Yard, Organic Garden, and carriage horse stables. Then it was back down the drive past the deodar and thatched Higher Lodge, and on through the gate to the old Totnes Road, where I turned left and came down the bottom of the steep hill to the centre of the village. There I was greeted by carriage driver Rick, who was having a brief coffee break: the inevitable exchange of jokes reaped its good humour rewards and left Rick's partner, Corinne, yawning. Just past the Old Granary Gift Shop I turned left into yesterday's farmyard with its old, gutted barns on the right. To the left was the rear of the Old Granary, next to the Weavers Cottage Tea Shoppe garden. Above it was Cockington Visitor Centre and Village Museum.

Coming through a small, ivy-clad arch, I walked up the gravel

The Drum Inn, Cockington.

Author

path with lawns on the left and the garden and hedge opposite. Before me was the handsome Drum Inn, which has a really classy look about it, from the dark, weathered, thatch roof and the windows, to the pale cream walls and brown-brick base.

Sir Edwin Lutyens, 1869 – 1944, was the famous architect responsible for the inn, which was completed in 1936.

To the left, on the lawn, was the beer garden for drinking only. But customers can enjoy their choice of the full menu on the patio picnic tables at the top of the broad flight of steps that saw me to the pub door.

Wandering into the interior, I found candelabra lights giving off a welcome glow. It was spacious, but cosy. To the right of the bar was the smoking restaurant, and, left of the door, the non-smoking restaurant. In the middle was the bar area. Main meals and snacks are available all day.

There were two real ales, four lagers, cider, Guinness, smooth ale, malt whiskies, and a good selection of wines. In the winter three log fires greet customers.

I brought my Wadsworth's 6X down to the beer garden and sat on the grass to listen to the songbirds competing with the laughter and chat of the groups at the picnic tables.

12. Torquay Harbour – Hope's Nose and back

Start and finish point: Torquay – Seamus O'Donnell's pub (SX 920 635).
Distance: About 5 miles.
Degree of difficulty: Grade B, some C.
Route: Seamus O'Donnell's pub, Victoria Parade, Torquay harbourside; Daddyhole Plain; Meadfoot Sea Road; Ilsham Marine Drive; the park; Hope's Nose and back.

Setting off from Seamus O'Donnell's, the pub on Victoria Parade, overlooking Torquay Harbour, I came left past the shops, cafes, and arcades. It was nearly noon in late September and really warm for the time of year. The sky was streaked with high clouds and vapour trails. I was wearing my usual summer walking gear.

Leaving the harbour, I came round the bend onto Beacon Hill, past the car park, public toilets, and Royal Torquay Yacht Club. Beacon Cove was down below. Then I stopped for a look at the sunlit view of the coast all round Tor Bay to Berry Head.

Striding on beyond Imperial Court, I turned right into the drive of the Imperial Hotel. The Coast Path sign was on the opposite side of the road and I came past the hotel's main entrance and The Villa to the three metal posts where the path narrowed. The sign on the left carried the tell-tale South West Coast Path acorn logo.

It directed me to the arduous section where I went up the steps – up and up. The angle was really steep. But at last a narrow footpath brought me down to a great viewing point of the Bay's south and west shoreline.

The rugged coast from Beacon Cove to Daddyhole Plain has many interesting features, like London Bridge, Thunder Hole, and West and East Shag, the offshore rocks.

With another steep descent the rough path went on, and soon I was walking through a copse of holm-oaks, that offered glimpses of some of the points, coves, and headlands. The next zig-zag steps climb emphasised that this part of the hike isn't for the unfit.

Ore Stone

Lead Stone

Hope's Nose

Thatcher Rock

Thatcher Avenue

Drive

The Park

Thatcher Point

Ilsham Marine

Meadfoot Sea Road

Meadfoot Beach

Walk 12
(not to scale)
B.C.

Daddyhole Road

Daddyhole Cove

Daddyhole Plain

Beacon Hill

Seamus O'Donnell's Pub

Imperial Hotel

Victoria Parade

Beacon Cove

TORQUAY Harbour

South Pier

Haldon Pier

75

Ever upwards I went until the path levelled out and passed through a crenellated stone tower on the clifftop. And on I walked past thickets of gone-wild fuchsia, draped with old man's beard.

There were benches with commemorative plaques, and the track was very rough and stony. But I was enjoying it. The Bay sparkled and I was on my way up another flight of steps which saw me through the shade and out onto Daddyhole Plain.

The sunny lawns were the tops. Standing there, swigging mineral water from the bottle, I could really appreciate those sea views, with the hills of Dartmoor inland to the right (west). In the nearby headland car park old couples sat in their cars, and moments later I was off again down the steps to the right of the car park, on the path leading to Meadfoot Beach.

The Coast Path was signposted at the bottom and it was down, down, down, through cool woodland where the path became narrower and the grey squirrels noisier. Then I was on Daddyhole Road where a giant conifer stood among the holms on the bend. Birds chirped close to the pay-and-display Meadfoot Beach car park.

Turning right onto Meadfoot Sea Road, I came down to the pavement past the impressive cream facade of the Osborne Hotel into a vision of Thatcher Rock, Ore Stone, and Hope's Nose. The pavement was next to the sea wall and the breeze coming off the tideline smelt fishy. Waves broke, and the star of the coastal scene was Thatcher Rock.

At Kilmorie car park, at the end of the prom, the Coast Path to Anstey's Cove was signposted. There the short, narrow path took me into Ilsham Marine Drive where I turned right to walk up under multi-storey Kilmorie Flats.

As a heretic hiker I'm happy on roads which aren't mad motorist rat-runs. Ilsham Drive was fine in this respect. Almost every gap in the trees on the right offered spectacular sea views; and at the top the rough little lawn, and its benches, was an ideal viewing point.

Then I was at the seven-and-a-half-acre park, overlooking Thatcher Point, for the climax of those Bay and Channel views. On the crew-cut grass I found a couple of strange, honey-coloured, toadstools, which turned out to be stale, discarded ring-doughnuts.

Presented to the community in 1968, by an anonymous donor, the park slots neatly into the Bay's coastal heritage. And I was glad to see Thatcher Rock in 3D against the glare of the Channel.

Around the bend, a bit further on from the park, I was above Hope's Nose. The footpath onto this Site of Special Scientific Interest begins at the metal stile entrance opposite the top fork of Thatcher Avenue. The SSSI is managed by Torbay Coast and Countryside Trust.

A moment later the public footpath, and narrow aisle through the blackthorn, brought me onto the Nose. My one-mile circuit was obvious and well defined. Where the path divided I went down to the right.

Oh, yes, and I was prepared to see some of the unusual animals which have become residents of the headland. They are the hardy, dark-fleeced Soay sheep, introduced to the site in 2003 by the Trust to help keep down the scrub.

Padding on, I didn't disturb the rabbits. Feeding close to the gorse and bramble thickets, they ignored me except for a brief clenching and unclenching of noses. Nearby a starling sounded like an Irish bar musician playing the soodlum whistle to perfection. The mellow tones were typical of that tin instrument.

A rock pipit flew by, bracken was shaking, and the broad, well-worn path had songbirds on it.

The popularity of Hope's Nose is understandable. But I never forget that it is a wildlife reserve, not a place to picnic on or do anything that will disturb the birds and animals in residence. I restrict my quiet visits to autumn and winter, beyond the breeding season of the birds.

During my hike I knew a lot was happening, from the scrub and rare flora-limestone grassland to the sea cliffs and rocky shore. Throughout the spring there are rich pick-ups for birds of prey and predators. Foxes take first-brood herring gull chicks from the rock terraces at the foot of the sea cliffs. But the bulk of the breeding herring gulls, thousands of them, escape the hunter by nesting on Ore Stone, Lead Stone, or Thatcher Rock.

Hundreds of kittiwakes, the occasional pair of lesser black-backed gulls, great black-backs, cormorants, shags, and guillemots also raise their young on the offshore rocks.

Coming up the path, I saw three or four Soay sheep watching me from the scrub to the right. A few more lifted their heads as I approached the tip of the Nose, where a bench provided a good view of Thatcher Rock. I then turned my lightweight binoculars on Ore Stone, about half a mile away.

Lead Stone 'appeared' as I strolled on for clifftop close-ups of the rocks and reefs exposed by the falling tide. Oystercatchers piped.

Walking the lower path was great. Thrift stirred in the wind. But I was admiring the classic view back across the Bay, with the houses of Paignton and Brixham close to the sea and on the hillsides. It's no accident that Devon rhymes with heaven.

On the tip of the Nose was a funny little coastguard lookout, and wandering around the disused limestone quarry I looked north to Black Head, with red cliffs all the way to Dawlish and Lyme Bay.

Apart from the outstanding coastal beauty, in the wildlife and wildflower context, a lot goes on at and around the SSSI, throughout the year. It's a lovely place.

Returning to my Hope's Nose starting point, the path rose steeply. But I wasn't in a hurry. I knew Seamus O'Donnell's would be open and the beer would be cold at the end of a very rewarding hike.

The pub is one of those taverns in town, up to date, but a place Dickens would have been happy to frequent. The bar has classy bar stools and alcoves with tables. The atmosphere is Irish. On the wall the old advert board read: 'The taste of Ireland. Kilkenny Irish Beer. None better since 1710'.

There is draught Guinness – extra cold, or straight, draught lagers, and ciders, as well as eight Irish whiskies, including Jamesons, Paddy, and Old Bushmills.

On the wall, behind the counter, the notice caught my eye: 'Irish Diplomacy – The ability to tell someone to go to hell so that he will look forward to the trip'. My Granny Kerry would have liked that.

'We have live music in the evening on Wednesdays, Fridays and Saturdays – and Sunday afternoons,' one of the friendly ladies behind the bar told me. 'And there's big-screen TV, the pool table, and kiddies area.'

As you come in the door the restaurant is upstairs on the left. But starters and main dishes can also be eaten downstairs. The bar snacks include pasties, burgers, sausages, and sandwiches.

'We also have a family room and a snug area to sit and smoke in', the lady added, as she showed me the upstairs beer garden patio, with its harbour views.

The lighting downstairs was low, and it was good to find pub food once again elevated to tasty restaurant meals. But I was happy on an alcove seat, with a pint of Caffrey's Irish Ale, and prawn Marie Rose sandwiches and side salad.

Seamus O'Donnell's, on Victoria Parade.
Courtesy of Seamus O'Donnell's

13. The Cider Press Centre Trail

Start and finish point: Totnes – The Royal Seven Stars Hotel (SX 805 604).
Distance: About $4^1/2$ miles.
Degree of difficulty: Grade A.
Route: The Royal Seven Stars Hotel; Totnes Bridge; the Dart Riverside Walk; the weir; Dartington Lane; water-meadows and woodland; Dartington Cider Press Centre; and back to the Royal Seven Stars Hotel.

The early March weather was at its best – sun, cloud, and the odd shower – and I was in Totnes, a Saxon town crowned with a Norman Castle and surrounded by tree-hackled hills. Full of character, the town also boasts medieval buildings in High Street and Fore Street, and then there's the 13th century Guildhall, Rampart Walk, the Poultry Walk, and Butter Walk.

Leaving the Royal Seven Stars Hotel, at the bottom of Fore Street, I crossed Coronation Road, not far from the Wills Monument on The Plains. On Totnes Bridge I came down the steps to

The Royal Seven Stars Hotel, Totnes.

Author

the left onto Riverside Walk. The tidal Dart was low and I was admiring the snowdrops and celandines in the grass to my left.

Black-headed gulls were on the water, the path had a thin coating of mud, and there were young trees each side of it. Safeways' car park was on the left, and two gangs of mated mallards were behaving like Shakespeare's Montagues and Capulets.

Approaching Brutus Bridge, I came down to the right, just before the road, and went under the bridge. A young mum on a

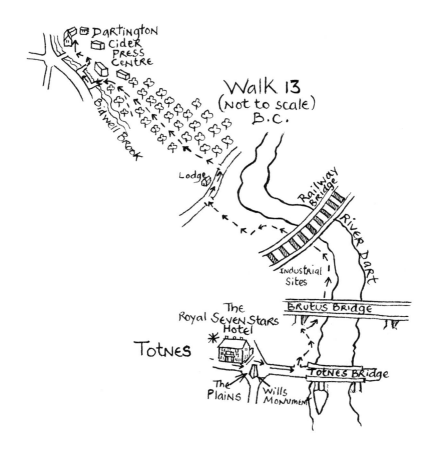

A section of the attractive Riverside Walk.

Chris Carter

bike, and her two little sons on mini-bikes, waved as they passed.

Then I could see the yards and warehouses of Totnes Industrial Estate. Across the water, meanwhile, a couple of crows touched down in a meadow, and a robin sang from the blackthorn blossom.

Daffodils were among the celandines beneath the trees, and the path had a real, finished hard surface because it is well used by cyclists and walkers.

Coming under the railway bridge, I turned left at the foot-bridge, past the Dairy Crest yard and its articulated lorries. There was a nip in the air and a cormorant messing about on the river.

I took the lower path to watch the gull gatherings and mute swan capers on the gritty sandbank. The tidal Dart ended at the weir, and in a little clearing, close to the path on the left, a chap was going through a series of slow-motion movements, like a genesis heron celebrating creation.

For a while I was dodging varicose roots and rocks on a very stony section of the path, before turning left then sharp right over the footbridge. Ahead was King Edward VI College sports field. And, after swinging right at the end of the bridge, I found myself on a broad, smooth, hard path.

That surface had been specially created as a level route suitable for all the community, including the blind, parents with pushchairs, wheelchair users, and cyclists. It's a credit to the South Hams District Coast and Countryside Service.

At the top of the weir it was right once more, beside a low wooden fence, to pass a small picnic spot and another picnic table and benches a bit further on, near some willows. Songbird skirmishes told me spring was close. But not much was happening on the wetland below.

Then I was leaving the footpath to turn right through the metal gates into Dartington Lane, which is the road leading to Dartington Hall. Beside the pavement was a line of tall oaks and a solitary beech. The old lodge was on the left, and a moment later I could look up the combe at the water-meadows. Sunlight gleamed on puddles and pools.

It was good to take the left-hand footpath that ran along the bottom of the woods. The Bidwell Brook divided the meadows, and the path was wheelchair and pushchair friendly.

Catkins, primroses, and celandines hinted at what the month can offer en route to spring. Behind the meadows were low, green hills, with sheep quietly grazing. Bonfire smoke drifted across the scene.

The wood was the local squirrels' gym. Trees stood high against the sky and the easy walking would have appealed to tots and octogenarians. Then I was overtaken by a bloke with long, black dreadlocks, a black goatee beard, long black coat, and black leather boots. His companion was a young lady with long black, green, and red hair; a long black coat, and black leather boots. Both wore sunglasses and were smiling like dreamy unicorn-spotters.

The woodland path went on, down to the old Mill House, where the waterwheel was turning, and over a small stone bridge. Coming past the mill, I crossed the wooden bridge for the left turn to bring me below the wood again. The Bidwell Brook was to the left and the path was shadowy. It took me into Dartington Cider Press Centre, thinking of a coffee and a bottle of Sheppy's Goldfinch Cider to take home.

The absence of people surprised me, though, as I passed the old limekiln and Tridias Toyshop. Then, walking straight on to Cranks Restaurant, I found everything was closed. A nearby notice told me the Cider Press Centre was open from Easter to Christmas.

Oh, well, I was happy to reverse the trail, more than ready for bar refreshment when I reached the Seven Stars.

Beyond the portico the Saddle Room Bar, with its low-beamed ceiling, was waiting. The name gave me a clue to the hotel's history.

As an inn it dates from 1675, and was a favourite haunt of merchants coming into town to trade at the market. In 1720 Daniel Defoe was a guest for a few days.

Seven Stars is a reference to the seven stars in the crown of St Mary the Virgin. There was once a chapel on the site, and in the Middle Ages religious houses were also hostelries. Saddle horses, and those pulling chaises and private carriages, as well as the stagecoach teams, enjoyed the luxury accommodation. The original name was the Seven Stars Posting House. Stagecoaches regularly left for destinations like Exeter, London, Plymouth, Falmouth, and Penzance.

Royal Mail coaches also arrived and departed on a regular basis. But all this profitable activity was killed off by the arrival of the railway in the 19th century. So the posting house became a hotel, which was very popular in Victorian times and the early 20th century for functions, dances, and … roller skating!

How do I know this? Well, it's all in *A History of the Royal Seven Stars Hotel*, a great little paperback, written and illustrated by Paul Presswell. Published about 40 years ago, copies were available at the hotel reception.

I made myself comfortable at a corner table close to the fire, while lunch customers arrived in the Carriage Room Food Bar, or the Brutus Room Restaurant, next to the Saddle Room Bar, where people were already ordering food.

The Saddle Room Bar was well endowed, drinkwise, from the Courage Best Bitter, John Smiths, and Carlsberg on draught, to bottled beers. The guest real ale was Rumpus, by Ridleys, and I was well satisfied with a pint of it, and a cheese and biscuits snack, while the more upmarket clientele sipped the bottled wines.

Apart from a welcome thirst, I had a flushed face, which a warm atmosphere produces after a few hours in the cold, fresh air – helped, of course, by a little alcohol.

14. The Teign Estuary Low Tide Trail

Start and finish point: Shaldon – The lower car park (SX 939 718).
Distance: About 5 miles.
Degree of difficulty: Grade A.
Route: The lower car park; the Ness House Hotel; Shaldon Bridge; Gravel Point; the Arch Brook; the Coombe Cellars Inn; and back to the Ness House Hotel.

The sun of early summer was shining on the Teign estuary when my friends dropped me off in Shaldon's pay-and-display lower car park, near the bottom of Ness Drive, just beyond Shaldon Wildlife Trust Zoo.

Walking down the narrow road, I passed the Ness House Hotel. This elegant Regency villa stands against the trees of The Ness, one of South Devon's most impressive headlands, there at the mouth of the River Teign.

As a hiker I was aware of the tidal problems. The walk should be started within 2 hours of low tide, and don't forget – on this trail there are muddy stretches. Strong boots are essential. Gritty sand, rocks, and seaweed are treacherous when wet.

Lingering briefly on Marine Parade, I could look across the water at The Point and Spratt Sand. Teignmouth's quays faced the tidal island called Salty. Beyond the estuary the town's houses covered the hillside.

Down on River Beach the easterly breeze had picked up. Metal rigging beat against the alloy masts of yachts on the shore; and soon I was passing the Shaldon – Teignmouth passenger ferry point.

I believe my trail had left the Coast Path and was following the Templer Way. Salty was on the right. The sandbanks, shingle, and mudflats are famous for their shellfish, seabirds, and waders.

But the outstanding feature of the estuary is Shaldon Bridge. The first wooden structure, completed in 1827, was once the longest bridge in England and the second longest in Europe, with Le Pont de Lyon, in France, beating it by just 28 feet. The 1,672 feet

of it had thirty-four arches, and its contemporary is an attractive aspect of the tidal Teign.

The Templer Way is named after James Templer, the Devonian who made his fortune in India, mainly through building the Madras Docks.

In 1792 his son, James, built the Stover Canal to carry clay for export from Teignmouth Docks; and in 1820 grandson George had the granite tramway constructed. It ran from Hay Tor to the canal basin so that the quarried granite could be taken to Teignmouth and shipped off to wherever the customer needed it.

Continuing along the beach, I came up the steps opposite Dolphin Court to walk the last part of the parade called Riverside. At the end of it was the left turn to the Church of St Peter the Apostle. Consecrated in 1902, this was one of John Betjeman's favourite churches. The poet was a fan of Gothic Revival architecture, and the interior is beautiful.

With maximum care I crossed Bridge Road onto the Embankment Path which saw me past the sports field and on to Ringmore Road. Then it was along the pavement to the right before another right turn at The Strand brought me to the foreshore. I was greeted by the muted cries of seabirds, estuary smells, and the sunlight flicker of swallows as the rough walking began.

On my left was the bushy greenery of the season. Soon I was crossing Gravel Point, to walk the long stretch of shore that brought me to the Arch Brook, where the stream spills into the river. At the bend on the road I came over little Arch Brook Bridge to return to the shore and walk on to Coombe Cellars and the Coombe Cellars Inn.

Anglers were on the tideline, and this is a popular spot for water sports fans and boating people, as well as the pub regulars and irregulars like me.

I had a look at the Templer Way noticeboard and the river views. Across the water, beyond Bishopsteignton, was traditional farmland with the Haldon Hills behind it.

The Coombe Cellars Inn is an historic riverside pub, and the ideal turning point on my five-miler. The distinctive white building is another famous feature of the lower tidal Teign, and it's seen a lot of trade since it opened in 1750. People come here for the good food, drink, and friendly atmosphere. The notice on the restaurant wall reveals that Nelson spent the night here with Lady Hamilton.

The inn has nautical knick-knacks in the bars, and adult dining areas with their low ceilings. Attractive as it all was I needed to get outside with my half of lager for a dose of sun and sea breeze. So that's what I did, to be greeted by the great beer garden terrace view.

Downstream was Shaldon Bridge, and on each side of the Teign were low, green hills. It was good to sit there in silence, enjoying everything, including the cool, blond beer. Meanwhile, kids from family groups headed for the Children's Play Area, and couples were catching the sun on the grass by the picnic tables. The mudflats gleamed between the sundazzle on the water, mated gulls soft-talked each other, and craft were at their moorings.

The inn's contraband connections aren't surprising, considering the site and that notorious haunt of smugglers, The Ness, which I had left about two-and-a-half miles downstream.

The owner told me about the Anglers' Floundering Competition on the shore in September and October. They can be seen along the edge of the tide, both sides of the pub. And pleasure boats visit the inn quay throughout the summer.

The estuary pageant continued as I departed to make my way back to Shaldon, relaxed, and notching up new views en route.

As inn outings go this one is rather special, with a good pub at the halfway mark and the Ness House Hotel at the end.

The House was built as a summer residence for Lord Clifford. A well-known landmark on the South West Coast Path, it was also the place where many smugglers' paths met.

Good food is served in the Terrace Restaurant and the Conservatory Brasserie. But, as usual, I was beer garden-oriented, and that lunchtime things were really buzzing. And, by the way, I had cleaned my boots before entering the bar.

Well, I wasn't surprised that my thirst was more demanding than my appetite. Except at the dinner table, food to me is fuel, and premium lager, or real ale, an elixir. Of course, I wouldn't say no to Ness House baked fillets of Brixham sea bass on a glazed

Bernaise sauce, or a local seafood selection with a lemon mayonnaise. But on my lunchtime inn outings I'm usually content with a pint and a bar snack.

With my Carlsberg Export I settled in the beer garden, round the corner, there against the headland copse. Songbirds darted in and out of the small, ornamental garden conifers. A fishing boat was entering the river mouth with its engine throbbing; and I sat on the edge of a picnic table for a vision of Teignmouth. Cloud shadows crept along the hillside below Holcombe Down.

Then, from the lawn below the conservatory, I could look over the water where the river met the sea. The panoramic view was something special.

Relaxed, I greeted my friends who had arrived to join me over a 'jar' before we headed for home. The driver was an amazing rarity – an Irish teetotaller, who was happy to sip coffee as we lowered the level of our lager.

After my walk on the shore I had something to celebrate.

The Ness House Hotel at night-time.
Courtesy of the Ness House Hotel

15. The Old Woods, Old Lanes, Olde Inn Circuit

Start and finish point: Churston Ferrers – The Olde Churston Court Inn (SX 904 564).
Distance: About $3^1/2$ miles.
Degree of difficulty: Grade D.
Route: The Olde Churston Court Inn; Churston Lane; The Grove; Churston Cove; Marridge Woods; Elberry Cove; Elberry Lane; Green Lane; and back to the inn.

The winter morning was frosty. I put the Olde Churston Court Inn behind me and left the village of Churston Ferrers to walk down the single-track road and along Bascombe Road, towards Brixham. Churston Lane (the public footpath) was to the left behind the gate, not far from the bend; and that was part of my route.

The sky was blue and larks were singing over the ancient farmland. A high hedge of blackthorn and hawthorn creaked in the sea breeze that was making the grey hazel catkins shake like neurotic caterpillars.

The old Devon banks were rich with plantlife. But the whole combe, sweeping seaward from Churston Court Farm's cider apple orchards to Ball Copse and The Grove, was a classic pastoral composition of drystone walls, hedges, and small fields.

Winter heliotrope flowered among the husks and dead stems of foxgloves on the verges. A wren sang, and the handful of skylarks continued to trill above the grassland.

Ball Copse was on the left, with The Grove a bit further on. The cold nipped my ears and I was crunching through the cat-ice on the footpath in the field beyond the gate where Churston Lane ended abruptly.

The trees to the left were the top part of The Grove. But at the bottom of the meadow I found a patch of common. Rabbits scampered off into the gorse and blackthorn. Herring gulls cruised overhead and starling flocks flew low over the big wood.

The Grove has a wealth of wildlife and plantlife. Among the sweet chestnut trees, oak, ash, and sycamore are lots of shrubs and wildflowers – according to the time of year. Bluebells cover much of the ground (in season); and the wood is habitat for foxes, badgers, grey squirrels, and roving roe-deer, as well as sparrow-hawks and woodpeckers.

There's considerable badger activity in the late spring when, at dawn or dusk, you may hear a strange crunching, crackling sound. That will be badgers eating bluebell bulbs like kids chewing gobstoppers.

The path ran through the trees and I came down the steps, under the ash and sycamore of the lower part of The Grove. Passing the holiday camp chalets, I turned left at the signpost marked: 'Churston Cove'. Although the descent was steeper, at least the steps were broad. Ahead I could see the hills of Torquay across the Bay.

The sound of small waves breaking was comforting, and I was confronted by a great view of the Bay. Fishcombe Cove and the Battery Gardens were on the right. Then a slippery, rocky stretch, along the top of low sea cliffs, saw me out of the trees and down onto the little beach of Churston Cove. On the right was Fishcombe Point, which is well known to botanists.

Among the wildflowers found on the limestone grassland were henbane, autumn ladies tresses, twayblade; ivy broomrape, Portland spurge, bastard balm, St John's wort, and the very rare little robin, a mini-cousin of ragged robin. The last time I saw little robin was at the end of the 1980s. But apparently it did bloom into the last decade of the 20th century.

Crossing the pebbles above the tideline, I climbed the cliff steps and paused for a breather. This gave me a chance to enjoy the view from the top.

After that I came along a wide path and on into the top of Marridge Woods, with Churston Golf Course on the left.

The walking on the South West Coast Path was good. But I had to be careful. There were surface stones in places, some concealed by the leaf mulch.

Coming between the small brick pillars, that had once supported a gate, I was even more cautious. The path had its varicose roots, as well as stones; and soon it had narrowed to wind down through the trees to the junction with another path near Elberry Cove.

I took the right-hand fork onto the cove's beach, to crunch across the pebbles. The ruins of the 19th century bathing station, on a little rocky outcrop to the right, below Marridge Woods, were a reminder that this was once the private beach of the aristocrats that lived at Churston Court. It was next to a small, stone pier.

At the far end of the cove I went up the steps, with their hand-rail, onto a well-used footpath. Then it was left to pick up Elberry Lane and go left again. Elberry Farm was in the opposite direction, down below, towards Broadsands.

Over the fields to the right were the houses of the south part of Broadsands. The grass was stiff and white on the verges, and I was loping up the lane to the metal gate and stile onto a narrow path, where I met an old soccer buddy of the late 1950s and early 1960s. We had played for the same team.

After a short chat, heavy on reminiscence, he suddenly said: 'Bri, you're just the bloke. Thinking about the good old days, when us starred fer United, what was Ernie's second name?'

'Ernie who?' I grinned, and left him chuckling there, after it had sunk in.

The smell of cow manure lifted off the farmland, and I listened to the gull talk as I passed the garden walls of the bungalows on the right.

The path was rough. The climb is long and can be dodgy in wet weather. It took me between the golf course grass, past the ash saplings on the verge. The late morning was loud with bird calls. The wayside sign read: 'Please beware of stray golf balls'.

The next metal gate opened onto a narrow country road with tall hedges and entrances to attractive properties like Star Mist. Then I was out of Elberry Lane for the swing left into Bascombe Road, before another left turn brought me along wide Green Lane, which is a quiet side road leading into Churston Ferrers.

The big bungalow gardens provided their songbird cameos before my sharp right turn to come down past Churston Court Cottage. Behind it was the tower of the Church of St Mary the Virgin, and on the left were the old barns, byres, and stables of Churston Court Farm. Around the bend the graveyard faced the church, from the other side of the road. I strolled into the car park of the Olde Churston Court Inn, to be greeted by the crazy laugh of a green woodpecker as it lifted off the beer garden lawn below the church tower. Then I dumped my muddy boots in my son's car and put on my trainers. Chris was walking to Galmpton and back.

Although the noonday sun had no warmth, I still fancied a pint of cool real ale. No stranger to the Court, I was happy to be between its old walls again, soaking up the history. A Grade 1 listed building, the upmarket inn was once a Saxon manor that eventually became the home of Sir Hugh Ferrers.

Over the centuries, before Sir Hugh settled down, it was groomed into a medieval masterpiece of interior design. And when Peter Malkin bought it, back in April 1991, he completed the classic with a flair our ancestors would have admired.

But this is second nature to a man who is recognised as one of the country's leading experts on medieval buildings, and has spent his adulthood saving many from demolition.

The Olde Churston Court Inn – externally *(above)* and internally *(below)*.
Courtesy of the Olde Churston Court Inn

Examples of this practical dedication are Westenhanger Castle, Hythe, Kent; and Boringdon Hall, Plympton, a Tudor manor which he restored and made into a leading hotel.

The Court interior, with its sensitive lighting, includes a baronial bar, huge open fires, and high- and low-beamed ceilings; old passages, a carvery, old stone mullion windows, and flagstoned floors; oak panelling, tapestries, armoury, inglenooks, attractive staircases, and mirrors.

The resident ghost is a monk that haunts the kitchen, which is no surprise considering the quality of the cuisine available.

There are five large fireplaces downstairs and one upstairs. The biggest is in The Armoury.

I liked the presence of vintage timber everywhere; and the tucked-away snug, with its solitary settle, was another of those Victorian touches on the medieval scene. The faint aroma of burning logs and the sound of music from the Middle Ages united past and present.

I noted the three lagers on draught, the four real ales, and some good wines and whiskies on the bar shelf. The fireplace was a real work of art.

Then I had a look round The Carvery as lunchtime customers continued to arrive. On the menu board was a long list of bar snacks, and the fresh prawns with Marie Rose sauce and smoked salmon had instant appeal.

There were many starters and a wide choice of main courses. But I went for the fresh prawns bar snack, the perfect mate for my real ale. Then I settled at a table in front of the bar fire and its giant hearth, with the crackle of burning wood bridging the centuries. I had twenty minutes before my son joined me.

Winter only served to accentuate the delight of the inn's grate happening, in that fascinating time warp; and I could think of no better way to complete the final episode of my 'Bar Trek'.

※ ※ ※ ※ ※

The Author

Brian Carter has been the *Herald Express* Country Columnist and artist for nearly 25 years. During that time he has been nominated for a major national RSPB – Esso Award for his ongoing contribution to conserving the British countryside and its wildlife. In 2005 he was joint runner-up and highly commended in the Environmental Journalist of the Year section of the EDF South West Media Awards. Then, in July of that year, Brian's novel, *A Black Fox Running,* was on the select list in *The Guardian's* national poll of classic books about the British countryside – he was in the company of Wordsworth, Thomas Hardy, Emily Brontë, Richard Jefferies, W. H. Hudson, Edward Thomas, and other famous writers.

The author of six novels, published throughout the English-speaking world, he has also written many non-fiction books, including *Where the Dream Begins, Walking in the Wild, Yesterday's Harvest,* and *Dartmoor, the Threatened Wilderness.*

His paintings have been exhibited in Paris, Germany, Vancouver, and the Royal Academy, London. But Brian is proud of being the first living artist to have a picture hung in Torre Abbey, Torquay. He also loves working for his local newspaper on a daily basis.

Brian Carter